ISLAM

THE PATH OF GOD

SUZANNE HANEEF

LIBRARY OF ISLAM

ii

Printed in the United States of America.

Library of Congress Cataloging-in-Publication Data

Haneef, Suzanne
Islam: The Path of God
  1. Islam. I. Title.
   BP161.2.J713   1996   89-7854
   297-dc20

ISBN: 0-934905-77-0

Published by
Library of Islam
PO Box 595
South Elgin IL 60177

Distributed by
KAZI Publications, Inc.
3023 W. Belmont Avenue
Chicago IL 60618
Tel: 312-267-7001; FAX: 312-267-7002

To all of you, my readers,
who are seeking to know about
the faith of
Islam
or who are searching
for a path of life,
I dedicate this work,
with a prayer
that it may be useful to you
in your quest.

CONTENTS

IN THE NAME OF GOD, THE COMPASSIONATE, THE MERCIFUL

INTRODUCTION

The little book you're holding in your hands was written by an American woman who accepted Islam in 1965. However, when I first encountered Islam in the mid-50's, I knew absolutely nothing about this religion or its followers. In fact, whatever I *thought* I knew—that Muslims believe in a pagan deity called Allah and that they worship Muhammad—couldn't have been more incorrect and absurd.

At that time, the Muslim presence in this continent was hardly noticeable and was limited almost entirely to foreigners hailing mainly from the Middle East and the Indian subcontinent. American Muslims were extreme rarities, who came into their new faith with very little support from any direction: there were very few Muslim communities and Islamic centers, a small and inadequate supply of literature and information about Islam, and a severely limited number of live role models to learn from. The critical question of how Islam could be applied by people living in the mainstream of American society without sacrificing any of its basic principles or teachings had barely been asked, much less answered.

But during the past three decades, all this has changed dramatically. The Muslim community is now firmly established in this continent; currently there are some 1500 mosques or Islamic centers in the United

States, and a large number in Canada as well. Muslims are found everywhere, even in the smallest places. They are making significant contributions not only to the religious and spiritual life of North America but in many other areas as well: politics, business, teaching, technology, research, medicine, and the social sphere.

Islam is generally thought of as an Arab religion. But the fact is that Arabs comprise only one-seventh of the world's Muslims. Indonesia has the largest Muslim population in the world, followed by Bangladesh, Pakistan and India. Some twenty or so million Muslims live in the People's Republic of China, and triple that number in the former Soviet republics. Thus, the Muslim population in North America represents the Muslim world in miniature. While it consists primarily of Arabs and Indo-Pakistanis, there are also significant numbers of North Africans, Iranis, Afghans, Turks, Bosnians and South-East Asians. And there is a steadily increasing number of American Muslims.

Still, in spite of this growing Muslim population, and the fact that Islam and Muslims are constantly in the news, many people in America know almost as little about Islam as I did a third of a century ago. We may imagine that we're getting a lot of information on the subject from the media, but much of what comes to us is actually *mis*information, which does nothing but reinforce prejudices and stereotypes.

Even now, at the end of the 1990s, I find myself constantly surprised by the unwillingness of people in the West even to consider Islam as a possible source of correct information. I'll give you just one example of this. Christians and Jews are deeply interested in biblical history and archeology. But with very few exceptions, they approach these subjects without ever consulting Islamic sources, which would unquestionably provide a wealth of authentic information. And I keep asking myself, When are the people of the West going to realize the treasure that Islam is and avail themselves of what it has to offer?

I'm sometimes asked what attracted me to Islam. To answer this, I must give a bit of personal history.

By the time I first began to hear about Islam, I'd parted company forever with my earlier strong Christian convictions. Not finding answers to the insistent questions I was struggling with (questions which you'll frequently encounter in this book), I stopped believing in God because the only God I knew about was unbelievable. It was simply impossible for me to come to terms with what I perceived His dealings with humankind to be.

But as time passed, I found a deep aching emptiness within myself where God had previously been. It then became clear to me that Islam offered something I desperately needed: absolute certainty and clearness of direction. As I came to understand the Islamic concept of God and His purposes for mankind, it was one that made complete sense to my mind and that I instinctively recognized as right. Islam's emphasis on the individual's relationship with God and its deep spirituality drew me like a magnet. And I knew I had to make it my own.

It's been a long journey from that state of knowing less than nothing to this point. But it's been a grand and exciting journey. It's taken me from inner emptiness, sometimes verging on despair, into the heart of a faith which I've found to be like an ocean in its depth and breadth. This journey has allowed me to recapture the spirituality of my childhood, and to taste the flavor and sweetness of Islam as a way of life in some of the Muslim heartlands. Summing it up, it's been a journey of coming to an understanding of the purpose and meaning of existence and of finding my own personal path to God.

This is a path which I feel so blessed to be a part of that I must share it with others—with you, if you're willing. I'm offering to be the tour guide on your journey of discovery of a faith which is as dear to life itself to millions of the world's people. The fact that some of these people may be your neighbors, friends, fellow students, co-workers, grocers, physicians, teachers or even your relatives may make this journey more real and personal for you as you try to look at things through their eyes.

Muslims are no longer "those people over there." On the contrary, they're *over here* and they're an integral part of our communities. This fact in itself demands from us the willingness to be open-minded and to replace prejudice, speculation and stereotypes with accurate information, which hopefully in turn will lead to tolerance and respect. And in the process we may find out how much Islam and Muslims have to offer us.

My approach to the subject is simple and direct, not scholarly. I've emphasized the concepts and high spiritual principles of Islam rather than its rules; this is not a how-to-do book but simply an overview. May God, your Lord and my Lord, the Lord of the universe and every creature in it, bless you and guide you as you read.

I
THINKING THINGS OVER

"*Where am I going? This society? The whole human race?*" These are questions which many of us today are asking urgently, deeply troubled about what we see happening in our world

Our concerns may be quite personal ones, centered around our own particular life situation. They may be general ones, related to the state of things as a whole—or both. For this is a strange and difficult time, a time when all the old values and traditions seem to have been cut out from under us without anything clear and definitive having been substituted for them. From every direction and every possible source, we're being bombarded by the newfangled ideas, values and behaviors of the New Age in which we live.

The New Age is an age with many interesting features. One of these is confusion. Great numbers of us no longer seem to have a clear sense of right and wrong, good and bad. Under the impact of too much personal freedom and the flood of new ideas and values, we're falling apart, frightened, uncertain, lost. After all, how is it possible to have certainty about *anything* when even the most basic, time-honored values are being called into question?

In comparison to earlier times, everything around us today seems upside-down and backwards. A great deal of what was previously considered right is now looked upon as outmoded, irrelevant or just plain dumb. At the same time, much of what used to be considered wrong is now accepted as right, normal and okay. Members of the older generation, like myself, still maintain our vision of what things were like in an earlier, simpler, less perplexing period. But when our generation goes, apart from people of strong religious faith, who will be left that still retains a clear vision of a saner, more stable society? That vision will have gone with the winds of change.

This turn-about in basic human values and morals has led to a steady unraveling of civilized standards and behavior, not only in the country but worldwide. Brutality, lust and all manner of other evils flourish around the globe; violence, vice and exploitation seem to have become the new order of the day. And fear hangs over the whole world. Those of us who are even slightly sensitive to the currents and energies around us realize that something is wrong—deeply, awfully wrong. And we carry the collective burden of humanity's pain and turmoil deep within our hearts.

Day by day the fear and uneasiness increases. Often we sense that we're at the edge of a terrible and dangerous abyss, surrounded by intense darkness. As the end of this millennium approaches, predictions of a worldwide Armageddon-like catastrophe haunt our minds. And how can it be otherwise when we sense deep within ourselves that things have gone so wrong that such a crisis is due? For each day, new and deeper holes appear in the social and moral fabric of mankind, and it seem obvious that when the holes become more than the fabric itself, it's past repair.

Why? you may be asking. *Why is our society, our world, so terribly disturbed? Why is there so much suffering, misery and evil on earth? Why is everything around us and inside us in such a state of upheaval?*

Why are the rates of crime, violence, sexual misbehavior, family breakdown, substance abuse and suicide mounting day by day? Why are there so many problems within my family, among my friends, or in my own life? Why am I so anxious, depressed, stressed-out, uncertain, unable to find any peace of mind?

These are all-important questions. I've thrown them out to you, not in order to make you uneasy, but because they're matters which we urgently need to address. Yet we seem unable (or perhaps unwilling) to put our finger on the cause. Social scientists spend years studying such issues, but even they often fail to understand the primary reason for this troubled state of affairs, much less what can be done about it. Why? One possibility is that in a secular society such as ours, the reason is one that few people want to admit or accept.

Can it be that we're all suffering because a critical something is missing from our society and world in our time? And is it possible that because of this missing thing, a huge emptiness exists in a great many people's hearts? Might it be that our attempts to fill this void, although without knowing what it represents, has resulted in our blind race for material solutions, material supports and material satisfactions, without taking into consideration our total human nature and its needs?

Then, we may further ask ourselves, can it be that the race to replace that vital missing element with material goals and goods has warped our spirits and, in turn, our values even more? To take this line of questioning further, is it possible that the drive for material props could be fuelled by an intense spiritual hunger, even starvation, which we try to fill in any way we can?

In my view, the essential thing we've lost is religious faith. Together with faith, we've also lost the fixed set of values and principles which guided the lives of peoples and civilizations before us, giving them stability, continuity and certainty. The prevailing materialism that's taken the place of faith has resulted in a misplaced trust in science and technology, which are good servants but bad masters. It's cheated us and robbed us of a sense of direction, both as individuals and as a society. On a deeper level, it's also deprived our spirits of the deeper, truer satisfactions they require.

While earlier responsibilities and rights went hand-in-hand, today freedom rules. This freedom is defined as the right to do what one pleases without accountability as long as it doesn't "harm" anyone—that is, as long as no criminal or civil codes are violated. But who's to decide whether a word or an action is harmful to others, or to our own inner selves? Without a strong conscience, firmly grounded in universal principles of right and wrong, it's easy for us to be cheated by the desires of our egoes, so that whatever we want to do seems all right.

Because of this loss of faith and the moral responsibility which it instills, another catastrophe has occurred: our society's loss of its clear understanding of the family as a God-ordained institution, to be upheld and supported by every possible means. Sexual enjoyment has become an end in itself, divorced from responsibility. Better methods of "protection" are offered as the solution for the host of problems this attitude has brought upon us, rather than encouraging responsibility for the consequences of our actions.

Our children and their well-being have become the first victims of this loss. Many of us grew up in disrupted families in which we never learned any positive parenting skills. Some of us want to be good parents but are so strapped financially that it's difficult to be. Others of us have given priority to a better lifestyle or a rewarding career. No matter what the reason, great numbers of our children are growing up without the emotional security, parental love and attention they require to be healthy. And the circle of deprivation continues from one generation to another. As a result, we've become increasingly a nation of emotionally crippled, dysfunctional people. Due to no fault of our own, many of us carry hollow spaces inside hearts which should have been filled with love and a sense of well-being from the moment of birth.

Another casualty of our lost sense of responsibility is the moral and spiritual training of our children. From a young age, they're bombarded by values, morals and examples which conflict sharply with any religious belief, and even with civilized standards. But young people who've never been taught morals and values other than material ones have no standards for distinguishing right from wrong or beneficial from harmful. Nor do they have any effective weapons for fighting against their own powerful impulses or the pressures coming from outside.

Science, which many people believe provides answers to all questions, has played a major role in eroding religious belief and traditional values. Many people today question the very existence of God, demanding "proofs," although strangely enough, we never hear of anyone's demanding proofs that God does *not* exist. Others, although believing in His existence, do not grasp His relevance, even to their own personal lives.

Although as a society we may give lip-service to belief in God, this is far removed from having certainty that He is in complete control of all things. According to our current thinking, a vague force called "Mother Nature" (or just "Nature") is responsible for running the natural world in an orderly, predictable fashion. But when something out of the ordinary occurs, something which we look upon as unpreventable, such as a natural disaster, it's viewed as an "act of God"—as if God were some sort of an intruder in the smooth, orderly running of the universe.

But without firm belief in a Supreme Being who is continuously involved with His creation, we human beings are spiritually and emotionally empty and deprived. We go through life uncentered, unfixed, and a prey to every wind that blows, without clearly-defined beliefs, values or goals by which to chart our path.

If you grew up with a religion and strong faith, you're one of the lucky ones. Many of us were never exposed to anything of the sort. Others were brought up with a religion but later outgrew it; we still believe in God but don't subscribe to any particular faith. Some of us may have looked into various religions without finding any clear direction. Others would like to believe but don't have any idea in who or what, or even where to look. And still others of us may feel that even if we knew what to believe, we're beyond all hope of salvation.

Whatever your particular case may be, it is critical for you to know that you were created by an absolutely merciful, loving Lord. He created you because He desired you to come into being, and He honored you by breathing into you something of His Divine Spirit.[1] No matter who you are or what you may have done, *that* fact alone gives you worth and importance. And He, your Creator, is asking you to connect with Him.

God is always there for you. He never leaves you; there's no way you can get rid of Him. All you need to do is reach out to Him. If He doesn't have any place in your life but you would like Him to, initiate the relationship. Call to Him, ask Him for help and guidance, pour out your heart and your needs to Him, tell Him that you love Him. For without being firmly bonded to our Source, we're hollow, empty creatures, easily crushed and destroyed by the difficult conditions surrounding us. Without belief in the purposefulness of our lives, we're likely to be in despair.

At the same time, you need a way, a path to walk upon to Him, a system for guiding your life. But, if you're not to be misled, it must be a true and correct one.

Islam, the faith of one-fifth of the world's people, is one among many ways claiming to be the truth. I'm talking about real Islam, of course, not the biased versions you hear about in the media or the Farrakhan variety, but the genuine, pure faith that goes back to Prophet Muhammad (ﷺ)[2] and the early Muslim community.

Islam, meaning "surrender" or "submission", is the original religion revealed by God from the beginning of human history. He revealed it through the first man, Adam (ﷺ), who was also the first prophet. Later, He revealed it through Abraham (ﷺ), the father of Judaism, Christianity and Islam. *"Abraham was not a Jew or a Christian, but rather he was a man of true religion, a muslim,"*[3] God says concerning him.

Still later, He revealed it through Moses (ﷺ), and afterwards, through Jesus Christ (ﷺ), the miraculous prophet who came to revive and purify it. And He revealed it for the last and final time through the prophet who established Islam as a world religion, Muhammad of Arabia (ﷺ), the most perfect of all mankind. And this final revelation contains God's unchangeable guidance for humanity up to the end of this world.

"I hear what you're saying," you may be thinking. "But exactly who's making the claim that Islam is the truth, and why should I believe it any more than in the claims of any other religion?"

Good questions, which you *should* be asking. Islam's answer to the first part of your question is, quite simply,

God Himself. This, and much more, is what He has to say about His final revelation:

> O mankind, the truth has come to you from your Lord. Therefore, whoever is guided, is guided only for his own soul, and whoever is in error errs only against it. (10:108)

> That which is revealed to you [Muhammad] by your Lord is the truth. (13:1)

> Those who have been given knowledge see that what is revealed to you [Muhammad] from your Lord is the truth and leads to the path of the Almighty, the Praised One. (34:6)

> By the Lord of the heavens and the earth, this is indeed the truth, as [much as the fact that] you are able to speak. (51:23)

But claims to being the truth are not to be taken lightly. In order to test this claim for yourself, please read on. Gather information, sift and weigh it all in your mind, and come to your own conclusion.

If you do conclude that this religion is the truth, then other conclusions follow: that in Islam's divine Message lies hope for ourselves as individuals and for mankind as a whole—indeed, perhaps the only hope; that nothing other than this faith that can cure the deep, devastating ailments of humanity; and that, without it, there can be no lasting solutions, no safety, and no way out of the life-threatening global crisis of our time.

II
ISLAM'S WORLD VIEW

"I bear witness that there is no deity except God,[4] and I bear witness that Muhammad is the Messenger of God—*Ashhadu an la ilaha illa-Llah, wa ashhadu anna Muhammadu Rasool-Allah.*"

Muslims repeat this Declaration of Faith over and over again in their daily prayers. But what does this Declaration really mean?

This act of witnessing proclaims that I accept no one as my God except the One, Eternal, Almighty God, who alone is worthy of my worship and service, and that I accept Muhammad (ﷺ) as His last and final messenger to mankind. In accepting both, I'm prepared to follow the guidance which God revealed through Muhammad (ﷺ) as my way of life and my path to salvation.

When a person is ready to make such a commitment, he or she enters Islam by repeating the Declaration of Faith in front of witnesses. He or she is now formally a Muslim, part of the world-wide community of the millions who live by the teachings of Islam. He or she is also absolved of all sins committed before accepting Islam, as pure as a new-born baby.

1 THE AGE-OLD MESSAGE OF ISLAM

I have already pointed out that Islam is not a new religion. Rather, it is the original religion revealed by God to mankind from the dawn of human history. Thus, the first man, Adam, who was also the first prophet, was a *muslim* in the sense of being surrendered to God. And after him came a series of prophets, including those we mentioned previously and many, many others, who were all *muslim*s or surrendered ones. And every single prophet brought the same divinely-revealed Message from his Lord.

And what is that Message? It is that there is a single, unique Being who is the Lord and Master of all creation. He alone deserves to be worshiped and obeyed, and we, mankind, are accountable to Him for all our actions. We are in this life for a brief, limited period, after which we will return to Him for judgment. We will then enter a life of eternal duration, during which we will either be in permanent happiness or in misery. And the choice of our destiny in that future life is up to us.

2 UNDERSTANDING REALITY

Now, everyone has a certain world view, an understanding of what constitutes Reality, and this view naturally differs greatly from person to person. But what's really important about our world view is whether it's a correct one or merely someone's mind-product—possibly our own.

If it's correct, well and good. However, if it's one that we human beings have concocted out of our own or other people's guesswork or imagination, it's bound to be wrong. On our own, we simply don't possess the equipment or capability to grasp what makes up this endlessly complex Reality. And since our principles follow from our world view and our actions follow from our principles, if our world view is wrong, everything we do is almost bound to be wrong as a result.

What we've got to figure out is this: Is Reality only what we can see, touch, taste, smell or hear with our bodily senses or grasp by means of our technology, or is there something more? Is there Someone in charge of it all who is Himself the Ultimate Reality, or are there just individual bits and pieces? Is everything in existence simply the result of randomness, coincidence or blind chance? Or, alternatively, did Someone arrange it so that all the bits and pieces are actually parts of a great, meaningful whole, an unbelievably grand, complex cosmic plan?

Then, if there is such a Someone, who and what is He? And—if you really want to take all this to its logical conclusion—isn't it just possible that finding out about that Someone is the most important thing anyone has to do?

Let's continue this line of questioning and get more personal. Perhaps we further need to ask: Does my own individual, personal life have any purpose and meaning, or not? Does it really matter what I do, say, think or feel? Am I just some physical being who will one day stop living, like all other living things, so that, suddenly, when the switch is turned from On to Off—*fini*? Is this life that I'm now in the only life, or was there something before it—and if so, what? And will there be something after it for me, some other state of existence? If not, none of these questions matter. But if there *is* going to be something after it, the critical question is: What is that future life of mine going to be like?

These are questions that every thinking person must ask because they form a vital part of human consciousness, questions which human beings have sought answers to since the beginning of history. The only problem is, *Who has the answers?*

3 ARRIVING AT ANSWERS

It's obvious that finite beings cannot arrive at answers to questions such as these on their own, for such questions are related to Infinity. Therefore, to rely on our limited senses, technology, thought processes or personal understanding for answers is futile and may even be dangerously misleading. For, again, even if some of our answers are right and some are wrong, the end result is bound to be inaccurate.

We are therefore faced with the unescapable conclusion that no one can possibly have all the correct answers except the One who created the whole. Only when the Creator Himself supplies us with the answers are they certain to be correct ones. Otherwise, human attempts to arrive at such answers are bound to be nothing more than guesses, or, at best, bits and pieces of the truth. And in view of our limited equipment, answers arrived at on our own probably have much more likelihood of leading us astray than guiding us aright.

Islam teaches that God, the Creator, Himself communicates the answers to us. By means of revelation through His chosen representatives, the prophets, God speaks to us about Himself and His creation. He informs us that there is an ultimate Reality which is known only to Himself, its Originator, and that He is the sustainer and center of that Reality.

What we human beings are able to know and understand of this Reality by means of our limited human equipment is actually only the tiniest, most minute portion of it. God refers to this part of His creation that we're able to know about or experience as the 'Witnessed' or visible, in contrast to the 'Unseen' or spiritual realm. And He makes it clear that belief in that unseen realm is a pre-requisite to being open to receiving His guidance, His final Message to mankind, the holy scripture of Islam known as the Qur'an, saying,

> *This [Qur'an] is the Book in which there is no doubt, a guidance to those who are mindful of God, who believe in the Unseen.* (2:2-3)

Anyone with a working mind is aware of the incredible complexity of the physical universe in which we live, as well as of our own selves. But it's quite probable that the complexity of this material world is as nothing compared to the infinitely greater complexity of the unseen Reality. Its depth and complexity is so immense that even the prophets, who were intimately connected to the spiritual realm, knew only a minute part of it.

It is therefore critical that we take our answers to the questions we've asked about Reality and about ourselves from the One who has them, not from any other source. Otherwise, we may never fulfill our appointed destiny and may end up in some limbo which we're not going to like. It's our business, our obligation as thinking human beings, to know the answers to these and many more questions which relate to our ultimate destiny.

We will start by taking a look at the basic beliefs of Islam, which are a summary of the unseen realities and our own place within them.

III
BASIC BELIEFS

1 THE ONE GOD

Belief in the One God, the Creator and Lord of the heavens and the earth, is the first basic article of faith in Islam. But in order for any of us to have a correct understanding of God, we must first arrive at an answer to our earlier question, Who and what is He?

THE NATURE AND ATTRIBUTES OF GOD

The following verses from the Holy Qur'an provide us with an understanding of the nature and attributes of God, the Most High. And the Describer is none other than God Himself, who has informed us about His own exalted Self in these words:

> *God—there is no deity except Him, the Living, the Eternal. Neither drowsiness nor sleep overtakes Him. To Him belongs whatsoever is in the heavens and whatsoever is on the earth. Who is the one who can intercede in His Presence except by His permission? He knows what is in front of them and what comes after them, and they do not grasp anything of His knowledge*

except as He wills. His Throne extends throughout the heavens and the earth, and He does not tire of guarding them; and He is the Most High, the Almighty. (2:255)

He is God, besides whom there is no god, Knower of the Unseen and the Visible; He is the Most Compassionate, the Most Merciful. He is God, besides whom there is no god, the Sovereign, the Holy One, the Source of Peace, the Guardian, the Preserver, the Almighty, the Compeller, the Supreme. Glorified be God above the partners they attribute to Him! He is God, the Creator, the Maker, the Fashioner. To Him belong the most beautiful Names, and He is the Almighty, the All-Wise. (59:22-24)

From these verses, we should easily be able to grasp that the Reality of God, the Creator and Ruler of all things, is great and exalted beyond human power to imagine or comprehend. For Almighty God, our Lord, is not some superhuman, bearded father-figure, a glorified man who sits on the clouds and orders creation by a wave of his physical hand. Rather, He is a totally unique, partnerless, transcendent Being who is not bound by any of the limitations of created beings. He does not possess a physical form or physical characteristics. He had no beginning and will have no end, nor does He have a father, mother, wife or children, or any other kind of 'kinship' with the beings He has created. As He proclaims,

He is God, the One, the Self-Sufficient. He does not beget nor is He begotten, and there is nothing comparable to Him. (112:1-4)

Originator of the heavens and the earth—how can He have a while He has no mate?[5] And He created all things, and He is well-aware of all things. (6:101; also 72:3)

They say, "God has acquired a son." Glory be to
Him — He is free of all needs! To Him belongs what-
soever is in the heavens and whatsoever is on the earth.
(10:68; also 2:116)

Thus, God Himself informs us that He is the All-Powerful, All-Knowing, All-Wise, Most Merciful Lord, the Originator, Fashioner, Sustainer and Ruler of all things in existence. He knows the most detailed workings of each atom of His creation, of every single part of the universe, all the secrets of life and death, and everything there is to know about ourselves, mankind. And He sustains and keeps everything in creation functioning according to His infinitely wise plan and laws. His is ultimate wisdom, power, skill and artistry.

To God belongs the sovereignty in the heavens and
the earth and whatsoever is in them, and He is power-
ful over all things. (5:120/5:123 in some translations)

Hence, it is clear that God Almighty is not like anything else, for only He is the Creator and all else is created. But even though, as Creator, He is totally unique and not to be compared with any of His creatures, nonetheless He is with His creation, all of it. At every single instant, *"He is with you wherever you are. And God is Seer of whatever you do"* (57:4). He knows the innermost secrets of our bodies, minds and hearts, and nothing whatsoever about us is hidden from Him.

We created the human being and We know what
his lower self whispers to him, and We are closer to
him than his jugular vein. (50:16)

And no deed do you do without Our being witness-
es over you while you are engaged in it. Nor does an
atom's weight in the earth or in the sky, nor what is
less or greater than that, escape your Lord, but is
[inscribed] in a clear record. (10:61; also 34:03)

At the same time, God Almighty is the possessor of the most exalted attributes, possessing all of them to the highest degree of perfection. Thus, as He is merciful and just, He is infinitely, endlessly merciful and just; since He is seeing, hearing and knowing, He is most perfectly, totally seeing, hearing and knowing; absolutely, unlimitedly powerful, and at the same time infinitely loving and tender. He is the Gracious, the Forbearing, the Forgiving; He is the All-in-All.

> *That is God, your Lord. There is no deity except Him, the Creator of all things; therefore, worship Him. And He is the Guardian of all things. (6:102)*

As the Sovereign and Lord, it is for Him to make any rules or laws that He deems suitable for His creatures. At the same time, because He is all-wise and all-knowing, any rules He makes for them are for their own good. He is the One who is accountable to no one but to whom all His servants are accountable. He did not create the universe and the creatures in it, including mankind, as a recreation or sport. Rather, He created them for the most perfect and just ends. And He created us, mankind, for a very special, high and extraordinary destiny.

GOD'S UNIQUE CREATION
—THE HUMAN BEING

"Who or what am I?" Possibly you may at some point have asked yourself this question. If so, you probably worked out some sort of an answer for yourself. *But—* and again this is of utmost importance—*how can you know whether or not your answer is correct?*

We will now turn to Islam's answer to this question, which has been provided by the Creator Himself. In the Qur'an, God informs us that among His many creations, we human beings are quite unique. While it is a fact that our physical bodies are similar to those of animals, we're not simply a higher form of animal life. For the thing that, more than anything else, makes us unique is that we possess immortal souls.

Islam teaches that our souls originated in the spiritual world. While we were in our mothers' wombs, they were put into our developing fetuses and came into this life with our bodies at birth. As long as we're here, our bodies are our souls' temporary homes—the places that have been 'leased' to them for a while, so to speak. Then, when the lease is up, our souls move out. When this bodily life ends, they return to the spiritual realm from which they came, prior to their final stop, their permanent destination. But we'll return to this point a little later.

Another thing that makes us human beings unique is that we have been given reasoning minds. Our minds work with our bodies and senses, sifting, analyzing, storing and transmitting knowledge. And still another unique part of us is the heart, not the bodily heart but the spiritual one, which feels, recognizes and understands at the spiritual level. The heart is allied with the soul, and has a desire and attraction for higher, spiritual things.

That brings us back to our bodies, which we all know about well enough. These bodies have specific material needs which must be met if they are to function properly: the need for oxygen, nutrition, sleep, sex, and all the rest. And allied to our bodies is our lower self, our ego, which is known in Arabic as the lower *nafs*.[6]

This *nafs* of ours has no use at all for anything higher. It's the grasping, greedy, power-hungry, primitive part of us which wants everything for itself and denies the rights of all others. By nature, it's purely selfish and, if it remains unchecked, can do evil beyond imagination. Its desires are endless, and the more one gives in to it, the more it demands.

All this tells us that our human nature is tremendously complex, a subtle blending of both interacting and opposing forces. The soul longs for God, for the spiritual life, while the lower self denies anything higher, has an unlimited appetite for worldly pleasures, and tries to stamp out the soul's yearning. Consequently, our bodies and minds can be used either for higher purposes or for lower ones, according to which side of our nature we permit to dominate. Likewise, our *nafs* can either be the force which enables us to carry out our responsibilities, or the power driving us to unspeakable evil. We have the capacity to be higher than the angels or lower than any animal.

THE ATTRIBUTES OF CHOICE AND RESPONSIBILITY

In today's world, a well-kept secret lies hidden amidst modern urban societies where technology appears to reign supreme. This secret is something that was universally known and unquestioningly accepted by people of earlier times, of simpler civilizations, and, still today, by many of those who live close to nature. If the rest of us don't know it, it may be, firstly, because we're in a state of denial. It may also be because we live with a great many illusions which we take to be realities. But when we're in the midst of a deadly storm at sea, when fire threatens to engulf our homes and ourselves, when an earthquake jolts the ground under our feet, when flood waters bear down upon us, or when a fatal illness comes upon us, the secret is out.

This secret is that we, mankind, are neither the masters of this universe or of our own beings, nor are we free. Rather, we are servants to God, bound totally by His Will. We do not own this world or anything in it, not even our own finite, perishable bodies; when we leave it, we'll leave with empty hands. Nevertheless, knowing our independent nature, God created us with the illusion of freedom, both so that we would not resent our servanthood to Him and so that we would have a chance to serve Him voluntarily. For, unlike animals or angels, we human beings have been created with free will—with the ability to make choices.

Animals, even the highest types, don't have a lot of choices about what they do, nor do they carry responsibility. But we, mankind, do; in fact, we were created for responsibility.[7] God tells us that He created human beings to be His vicegerents or stewards on this earth,[8] and stewardship is solely about responsibility. And responsibility, in turn, is about making correct choices with the wills that we've been given.

But although God created us for His own very special purpose,[9] we, mankind—inspired by the low desires of our *nafs* and by Satan—imagine that we've been put here to eat, drink, play and have a good time. A few of us are willing and faithful servants to God. But the majority of us—although imagining that we are free—become the slaves of a variety of masters. These masters are our own *nafs* (which is the most demanding master of all), its passions, Satan, and this world's attractions.

THE LAW OF CONSEQUENCES

It is hardly necessary to mention that all choices, and the actions which are the result of those choices, have consequences—good consequences or bad ones. In fact, this is part of the way we train our children: "You do this and *that* will be the result. You do that and you can expect *this* to happen."

Thus, while we have the freedom to exercise our wills as we like, we must know that every choice has consequences. We say, "I decided to do this," and then we follow a certain course of action. At the same time, God may be saying, "Yes, My servant, you are free to use your will. But I too am free. And the action of your will has set in motion consequences according to *My* Will." Therefore, our success or failure in this life and the Hereafter obviously depends largely on the choices we make.

What determines the choices individuals make? What is the critical factor in whether or not we're able to carry responsibility well? A lot of it has to do with the most basic and important choice of all: who or what we've chosen as the center of our life.

Our choice in this matter determines the kind of life we'll live: a God-centered or a Me-centered life. Will I listen and respond to and obey the guidance of my Creator, or will I be guided by my own whims and desires, following the dictates of my lower self? This is the all-important question whose answer each of us must decide for ourselves.

Again, God does not force us to acknowledge Him, worship Him, serve and obey Him. Instead, He asks us to use our freedom of choice to *voluntarily* choose to do so. In other words, the correct use of our will is to choose to accept and obey God's higher Will instead of our own often misleading and harmful desires. It is to surrender to Him instead of fighting against Him. It is to take Him alone as Lord to the exclusion of everything else that human beings worship.

For the fact is that each of us has a god of some sort, whether with a capital "G" or a small "g". Even people who claim that they don't believe in God have some center and focus of their lives, something they live for, something that's most important to them.

Perhaps you've never thought of the things that people live by or live for as their gods, but that's actually what they are. To check out this point, let's have a look at the definition of the word "god" in various dictionaries. For a start, *Webster's New World Dictionary* defines a "god" as "a person or thing deified or excessively honored and admired." *The American Heritage School Dictionary* defines a "god" as "something considered to be of great value or importance." *The Funk and Wagnalls Standard Dictionary* lists, among the definitions of the word, "Any person or thing exalted as the chief good, or made an object of supreme devotion," and "Anything that absorbs one's attentions or aspirations: Money is his *god*."

Would that include, for some of us, wealth, possessions, ambition, power, fame, work, science, art, technology, sports, fashion, appearance? Important religious, political or financial figures, sports or entertainment heroes? Maybe food, sex (of one kind or the other), having a good time, or things we're addicted to, such as drugs, alcohol, tobacco, TV, computers, entertainment, music, and so on? For some, maybe violence or even crime? And for many of us, our chief god may be ourself: *my* wishes, *my* feelings, *my* needs, *my* choices, *my* ideas, *my* decisions, *my* desires,[10] so that the primary object of devotion is *Me*. And in this case, it becomes very difficult for us to acknowledge or accept anyone as being more deserving of our devotion and service than our own all-important selves.

If we're really honest, we have to admit that any or all such objects of devotion fall under the above definitions of the word "god". And this leaves us with only two alternatives: either our God is God, our Creator, or it's a false god (or gods) of our own choosing.

Naturally, all of us live by some sort of principles, good or bad. Based on the above, it's clear that the choice of whom we take as our God determines the principles we live by. And our principles in turn determine the direction and quality of our life, and everything we do.

In the Western world, we talk a great deal about freedom. Some of our freedoms are tremendously precious and beneficial, and we're extremely fortunate to possess them and must know how to value them.

However, much of our so-called freedom is simply freedom for our lower selves to do whatever they want without restraint. But we're deceiving ourselves if we imagine this to be real freedom. In fact, it's simply another form of slavery.

But if we're after true freedom, not make-believe freedom masquerading as the real thing, it's important to understand that real freedom consists of being free from enslavement to all worldly masters. And that can happen only when we voluntarily enter into servitude to the one Master who is entitled to our service and worship, God Most High in His endless glory and perfection. To be the willing servants of such a Lord is the highest honor and rank we can ever hope for. Therefore, to attain knowledge of Him, to serve Him as well as we can, and to come close to Him through acts of worship, devotion and goodness is the highest goal we can aspire to.

2 THE ANGELS

Belief in angels is the second basic article of faith in Islam.

Today, we're seeing a lot of material published on the subject of angels. But we must ask, What is the source of this information, and how can we know if any of it is correct? Therefore, let us look at the Qur'an and see what the Creator of angels says concerning them.

> *Praise be to God, Creator of the heavens and the earth, who made the angels messengers with wings, two and three and four. He adds to the creation as He wills. Indeed, God has power over all things.* (35:1)

With these words, God positively assures us that angels really do exist. Belief in them is essential because they are a part of the unseen spiritual world which interacts intimately with mankind. The fact that there are at least eighty-one references to angels in the Qur'an shows how very important angels are. God says:

It is not righteousness that you turn your faces toward the East and the West [in prayer]; but rather, righteousness is that one believes in God and the Last Day and the angels and the Scripture and the prophets. (2:177; also 2: 285)

O you who believe, believe in God and His Messenger [Muhammad], and the Scripture which He revealed to His Messenger and the Scripture which He revealed previously. And the one who disbelieves in God and His angels and His scriptures and His messengers and the Last Day has surely gone far astray. (4:136)

From the Qur'an and Prophet Muhammad's sayings (*hadith*) concerning them, we know that angels are an order of spiritual beings, different from humans, whom God created from light. They have intelligence but do not possess free will as humans do. They worship, obey and serve their Lord without ceasing, acting as His agents and emissaries throughout the universe and among mankind.

God chooses messengers from among the angels and from among mankind. Truly, God is All-Hearing, All-Seeing. (22:75)

Among the specific angels we've been informed about is the angel in charge of rain, the angel who takes the souls of people at death, and the angel who is the keeper of Hell. One of the highest ranking among them is the archangel Gabriel (Jibreel in Arabic). It was through Gabriel (صلى) that God conveyed His revelations to the prophets.

At each moment, countless angels are glorifying their Lord and praying for His mercy upon mankind.[11] And each of us has two angels accompanying us throughout this life, recording our deeds up to the moment of our death.[12] It is this record that will be pre-sented to each of us on the Day of Judgment.[13]

Angels are normally invisible to human beings but when God wills they may be seen. According to Islamic belief, human beings do not turn into angels when they die. Angels are angels, and humans, even after death, remain humans.

Still another species of intelligent beings about whom God has informed us are *jinn*, whom the All-Wise Lord created from fire.[14] Like mankind, *jinn* possess free will. Some *jinn* are good—in fact, some are Muslims[15] — and some are evil. God informs us that Satan is the chief of the evil *jinn*[16] (not a fallen angel), whose task it is to tempt mankind to disobey Him.

3 THE REVEALED BOOKS

The third fundamental article of belief in Islam is in holy books or scriptures, revealed by God to certain prophets to convey His guidance.

> *We surely sent Our messengers with clear proofs and sent down with them the Scripture and the Balance [of right and wrong], in order that mankind might stand firmly for right.* (57:25)

THE EARLIER SCRIPTURES

The prophets who received sacred scriptures from their Lord were Abraham, Moses, David, Jesus and Muhammad, peace be upon them all. No traces remain of Abraham's Book. It is possible that bits of the Book revealed to Moses (ﷺ) may be found in the Old Testament books of Genesis, Exodus, Leviticus, Numbers and Deuteronomy (the Torah). Portions of the Book revealed to David (ﷺ) may be found among the Psalms. And parts of the Book revealed to Jesus (ﷺ)

may be found among the four Gospels of the New Testament.

However, there is simply no way to know what parts of these books of the Bible formed the original revelations from God, and what people added or subtracted later. Therefore, Muslims do not regard any part of the Bible in its present form as authentic and reliable. The Old Testament in particular is not a book which deals in sublime spiritual truths or in which prophets are depicted as towering spiritual figures. Rather, it is primarily a history of the Children of Israel. The God of the Old Testament seems much more like the semi-human, tribal deity of the Israelites than the All-Powerful, All-Wise, Most Merciful Creator of the heavens and the earth and everything in them, who is endlessly involved in every aspect of His creation. As for the New Testament, we'll examine its teachings a little later when we discuss Jesus (ﷺ).

THE HOLY QUR'AN

In contrast to all other scriptures which are claimed to have been revealed by God, the Qur'an is the only one which has been preserved in its original form. God says concerning it,

> *Truly, We have revealed the Reminder [the Qur'an],*
> *and We are surely its Guardian.* (15:9)

The Holy Qur'an was conveyed to Prophet Muhammad (ﷺ) by the Angel of Revelation, Gabriel (ﷺ), who received it from his Lord.[17] Over a period of twenty-three years, Muhammad (ﷺ) saw Gabriel (ﷺ), conversed with him,[18] and learned the verses of the Qur'an from him as they were being revealed. The angel also informed the Prophet (ﷺ) of the ordering in which the verses were to be arranged, as they remain up to the present time.[19] Addressing Muhammad (ﷺ), God says:

> Say: "The Holy Spirit [Gabriel] has revealed it
> from your Lord with truth in order to strengthen those
> who believe, and as guidance and good news for the
> Muslims." (16:102)

> And truly, your Lord is the Almighty, the Most
> Merciful, and truly, it [the Qur'an] is a revelation from
> the Lord of the universe, which the Trustworthy Spirit
> [Gabriel] has revealed to your heart, so that you may be
> one of the warners, in the plain Arabic language.
> (26:191-195)

As soon as the Prophet (ﷺ) received the verses from
Gabriel (ﷺ) and memorized them, he would repeat them
to his scribes, who wrote them down. In addition, many
of the first Muslims memorized the verses as soon as
they heard them; a number of these early Muslims had
memorized the whole Qur'an during the Prophet's lifetime. The entire Qur'an was also preserved in writing
during his lifetime, and it has come to us in the same
form, without any change.

THE CONTENTS OF THE QUR'AN

Much of what is contained in the Qur'an, no human
being could possibly know except through divine revelation. First of all, the Qur'an contains great numbers of
verses in which God speaks of His own attributes and
His all-wise divine plan. In the most powerful, moving
language, He informs us of His infinite power and creativity, of the human being's relationship and responsibility to Him, and of the certainty of the coming of the
Day of Judgment and the Life Hereafter.

Some of the Qur'an's verses also contain information
about the natural world which no one knew until cen-
turies later, a definitive proof of its divine origin. For
example, two verses speak about the orbiting of the sun

and the moon:

> It is not for the sun to overtake the moon, nor for
> the night to outstrip the day. And each one floats along
> in an orbit. (36:40; and 21:33)

In other verses, the Creator of all things gives star-
tling information about the formation of the universe
and the origin of life:

> Have not those who disbelieve seen that the heav-
> ens and the earth were joined together as a single piece,
> and then We parted them? And We created every living
> thing from water. Will they not then believe? (21:30)

> And God created every animal from water. (24:45)

In several verses, such as the following, the All-
Knowing Lord also details the development of the fetus
in the womb in a manner which exactly corresponds to
our present-day knowledge:

> We surely created the human being from an extract
> of clay. Then We placed him as a drop in a secure lodg-
> ing-place. Then We made the drop into a clot; then We
> made the clot into a lump; then We made the lump into
> bones; then we covered the bones with flesh. Then We
> brought it forth as another creation. So blessed be God,
> the best of Creators! (23:12-14; also 22:5 and 40:67)

Thus, in the Qur'an, we do not find any conflict
between reason and revelation. In fact, God speaks at
length about His creation, urging human beings to study
it and reflect on the greatness and wisdom of its Creator.
This urging to observe, reflect and discover the divine
wisdoms in creation later became the inspiration and
impetus for the extraordinary scientific development of
various Muslim peoples.

·   In His Holy Book, God also prescribes the Islamic acts of worship, so that we can worship Him as He Himself desires to be worshiped. Moreover, He establishes the moral and ethical principles for governing human conduct, as well as the practical rules of human interaction for both the individual and the society.

In the Qur'an we also find the stories of many earlier prophets and their people—something else no one could possibly know accurately apart from divine revelation. These stories were revealed as an encouragement to belief and as a warning against disbelief and denial of God and His messengers. Many matters related to the first community of Muslims—those who were alive while it was being revealed—and what they were passing through are also contained in it.

THE ROLE OF ARABIC IN ISLAM

Since the Qur'an, which is the direct speech of God, was revealed to the Prophet (ﷺ) in Arabic, it is always recited in Arabic during the Islamic prayers (*salat*) and at other occasions. However, renderings into all major languages are available for those who do not read Arabic. But since no one can "translate" the speech of God, these are not actually translations but are rather approximations to its meaning.

Those who know Arabic emphasize the tremendous power of the Qur'an's language and style. No rendering into another language can come anywhere close to the eloquent, earnest, moving power of the original Arabic, or do it the slightest justice. Neither can it be compared to any human speech or writings; in fact, it is well-known that the sayings (*hadith*) of the Prophet (ﷺ) himself do not resemble the Qur'an in style or language. Consequently, non-Arabic-speaking Muslims often make considerable efforts to learn to read and memorize parts of the Qur'an in Arabic.[20]

It certainly isn't necessary to know Arabic to be a Muslim. However, when a person accepts Islam, he or she will gradually become familiar with the sound of the Qur'an and with Islamic greetings and expressions, and little by little will memorize some verses or short chapters (*surahs*) to use during prayers. In fact, new Muslims are often eager to learn Arabic in order to be familiar with the power and majesty of God's Book, and to be able to converse and to understand other works in Arabic.

4 THE PROPHETS
AND MESSENGERS OF GOD

Belief in God's prophets and messengers is the fourth article of faith in Islam.

Islam recognizes two kinds of divinely-appointed leaders: a prophet (*nabi*)—one who brings a revealed message from God, and a messenger (*rasool*)—one who brings a message from God together with a divinely-revealed scripture. As mentioned earlier, Abraham, Moses, David, Jesus and Muhammad, peace be upon them, were all given sacred Books revealed by their Lord.

Although God gave certain knowledge of future events to prophets, the Islamic understanding of prophethood is not actually related to prophesying the future. Rather, prophethood is the highest rank of spiritual leadership and authority that God bestows upon mankind. No one can become a prophet by willing or trying to be, for prophethood is granted solely by God.

Thus, the prophets and messengers were men specially chosen, trained and prepared by God to receive and convey His guidance. They were the most perfect among mankind, reaching the highest moral and spiritual ranks. No other human beings have reached such a level.

Because the hearts of the prophets were always connected to their Lord, they were open to and capable of receiving His guidance. Each of the prophets spoke through God and for God; His words issued from their mouths by divine revelation and inspiration. In whatever they did, they manifested His divine Will, not their own personal human wills. Thus, they were, from the first to the last, *muslims*—that is, surrendered ones. And the Message they brought was nothing other than *islam*, or surrender to God.[21]

Prophets were sent to their people both as warners and as bringers of good news. The good news was of God's mercy and forgiveness, and of eternal Paradise for those who obey and follow His guidance. The warning concerned accountability to God, the certain coming of the Day of Judgment, the resurrection of the dead, and the terrible end awaiting those who deny their Lord's messengers and reject His guidance.

Prior to the coming of Muhammad (ﷺ), the last in the prophetic line, all the earlier prophets brought God's guidance to the people among whom they lived. This includes Jesus (ﷺ), who was sent to his own people, the Jews. Only the Message brought by Muhammad (ﷺ), the Seal of the Prophets, was for all people, of all places and times up to the end of the world.

We will now take a brief look at some of the most important prophets and their achievements.

ADAM (AADAM)

Adam (ﷺ) was the first man, created by God in Paradise, together with his wife Eve (Hawwa). Because the two were pure, innocent beings, Satan was able to deceive them and trick them into using their human attribute of free will to disobey God's command. They immediately repented of their sin—the personal sin of two individuals, not of a whole species, and a sin of heed-lessness, not of rebellion—and their Lord freely forgave them. But He sent them to earth to live out their des-tined term before returning to Him.

God appointed Adam (ﷺ) as the first in the line of prophets. Thus, the first man[22] and ancestor of us all passed on knowledge of his Lord and His guidance to his children. But presently the clear knowledge of God and obedience to His commands was replaced by idol-wor-ship and corruption. And God sent prophets, one after the other, 124,000 in all, to the various peoples of the earth.

The prophetic chain continued with such well-known prophets as Noah, Abraham, Isaac, Ishmael, Jacob, Lot, Joseph, Job, Moses, Aaron, David, Solomon, Jonah, Elijah, Zachariyah, John the Baptist and Jesus, peace be upon them all. Relevant parts of their stories are told in the Qur'an, as well as the stories of three additional Arabian prophets, Hud, Saleh and Shu'aib (ﷺ). And every single one of these prophets brought his people the same Message of submission and obedience to God.

The five greatest prophets in Islam, known as people of outstanding determination, are Noah, Abraham, Moses, Jesus and Muhammad, may God's peace be upon them. The outline of their histories follows.

NOAH (NUH)

Noah (ﷺ) is the first prophet after Adam (ﷺ) whose identity is clearly known. By his time, society had become corrupt and his people worshiped idols. God sent him among them with the Message of His Oneness, call-ing them to repentance and reform.

Noah (ﷺ) remained among his people for an extremely long period of time, exhorting, preaching and warning. However, they ridiculed him and those who believed with him, rejecting their Lord's guidance and finally making threats against him.

At God's command, Noah (ﷺ) and the few believers built a huge ship in the midst of dry land. When it was complete, God instructed His prophet to put into it a male and female pair of each kind of animal. Then, when His command came, Noah was to embark in it with the believers.

Finally, when the unbelievers had reached the peak of wickedness and hostility, God opened the springs of the earth and at the same time sent down torrents of rain from the sky. The flood water rose until no dry land remained. Noah (ﷺ) and the believers were safe in the ark, while all the unbelievers drowned, in spite of seeking safety upon a mountain.

After a time, at God's order, the flood water subsided. Noah (ﷺ) and the believers then left the ark[23] and began the process of rebuilding. A period of righteousness and belief in God followed, until corruption and idol-worship again became prevalent.

ABRAHAM (IBRAHEEM)

As we saw previously, Abraham (ﷺ), one of the greatest of all the prophets,[24] is the spiritual ancestor of Jews, Christians and Muslims alike. God says concerning Abraham (ﷺ), *"He was a man of true religion, a muslim"* (3:67)—that is, a totally surrendered one. Although his Lord tested him with the hardest of tests, Abraham (ﷺ) pleased his Lord so greatly in all of them that *"God took Abraham as His friend"* (4:125).

Because of Abraham's unswerving devotion and total submission to Him, God honored him by making him the ancestor of a long line of prophets. All the Israelite prophets were descended from him through his second son, Isaac (ﷺ). And from the line of his first son, Ishmael (ﷺ), came the most honored prophet of all— Muhammad, God's peace and blessings be upon him and upon them all.

MOSES (MUSA)

The life-history of the prophet Moses (﷽) has been
told in the Qur'an in greater detail than that of any
other prophet. It includes his birth and miraculous res-
cue from death at the hands of the oppressive pharaoh
of Egypt; his call to prophethood at Mount Sinai; his
going with his brother, Aaron (﷽), at God's command, to
call Pharaoh to repent and release the enslaved
Children of Israel; the Israelites's escape from death by
the act of God; the revelation of the original Torah, God's
Sacred Law for the Israelites; and the experiences of
Moses (﷽) and the Israelites in Sinai.

Moses's story has been told in such detail as a warning of what happens to arrogant oppressors and as an
evidence of how God supports His chosen prophets in
spite of anything anyone may do, aiding them by His
intervention when necessary. Moses (﷽) emerges as a
tremendous spiritual leader, struggling against all odds
in obedience to God's commands.

JESUS ('ISA)

No one can claim to be a Muslim without holding
Jesus (﷽) in the highest honor and respect as one of
God's greatest prophets. Indeed, Jesus's very nature was
miraculous, for God states in the Qur'an that he was
born of a virgin mother, Mary (Maryam), by His divine
power[25] and that he performed miracles by His permission.[26] But that does not mean that Jesus (﷽) was
divine any more than Adam (﷽), who was created without either a father or a mother, was divine.

> *The likeness of Jesus in front of God is like that of
> Adam. He created him [Adam] from dust and then He
> said to him "Be!" and he was.* (3:59)

However, the notion of God's having a son, wife, or

any other partner in His Godhood is totally contradicto-
ry to the reality of our Lord's Oneness, Uniqueness and
incomparable divine nature. Likewise, there can be no
"Spirit" of God which is other than God Himself.
Concerning these concepts, God says,

> *O People of the Book,[27] do not commit excesses in
> your religion, nor say anything except the truth about
> God. The Messiah, Jesus, son of Mary, was nothing but
> a messenger of God and His Word ["Be!"] which He
> bestowed upon Mary, and a soul created by Him.[28]
> Therefore, believe in God and His messengers, and do
> not say "Trinity." Cease! It is better for you. God is only
> one God. Glorified be He above His having a son! His
> is whatsoever is in the heavens and whatsoever is on
> earth, and God is sufficient as a guardian.* (4:171; also
> 6:101; 19:35; 43:59)

Such notions are also contrary to the actual teachings of Jesus (೫) himself. As a true prophet, he emphasized that God alone is the Lord and that only He is to
be worshiped and obeyed. Never did he direct anyone to
worship himself as a deity in place of or in addition to his
God, the Most High.

> *They who say, "Truly, God is the Messiah, son of
> Mary," surely disbelieve, for the Messiah [himself]
> said, "O Children of Israel, worship God, my Lord and
> your Lord." Indeed, whoever joins partners with God,
> God has forbidden him Paradise and his abode is the
> Fire, and there will be no helper for the wrong-doers.
> They who say, "God is the third of Three," surely disbe-
> lieve, for there is no deity except the One God. . . . The
> Messiah, son of Mary, was no more than a messenger;
> many were the messengers who passed away before
> him. And his mother was a woman of truth; the two of
> them used to eat food [like other human beings]. See
> how We make clear to them Our signs; then see how*

turned away they are [from the truth]! ([5:72-73, 75/5:75-76, 78 in some translations; also 5:17/5:19; 5:116-117/5:119-120)

Thus, if we are not to doubt God's words, it is clear that Jesus (ﷺ) never attempted to found a new religion with himself as its head, or—God forbid!—claimed to be a partner to his Lord or to be God Himself.[29] Rather, his mission was to confirm the original religion of surrender to God brought by Adam, Noah, Abraham, Moses and all the other prophets, peace be upon them, and to give tidings of the Last Prophet (ﷺ).

> *And when Jesus, the son of Mary, said, "O Children of Israel, I am surely a messenger of God to you, confirming whatever is in your hands of the Torah and giving good news of a messenger to come after me, whose name will be Ahmad."*[30] *(61:6)*

The Islamic understanding of Jesus (ﷺ) as a prophet rather than as God or the Son of God corresponds to the understanding of the early, original Christians. As is known by Biblical scholars, after Jesus's time, pagan notions were added to the pure Message revealed to him by his Lord, whereby he was 'transformed' into God/the Son of God and the third person of the Trinity.

But then, what about Jesus's crucifixion and resurrection from the dead? Since a great deal depends upon the correct answer to this question, let us see what God says concerning it:

> *And they did not kill him nor did they crucify him, but it appeared so to them. . . . They surely did not kill him; rather, God raised him up to Himself. And God is Almighty, All-Wise. (4:157-158; also 3:55)*

This statement is quite definite and emphatic, leaving no room for doubt. The Muslim's understanding is that, although it appeared to people that Jesus (﷽) had been crucified, God raised him up to Himself without his experiencing death. Jesus (﷽) remains alive in the spiritual world and, at a time known only to God, he will return to this earth. Here he will complete his special mission and here he will finally die. This is clear from the saying of Jesus (﷽) himself:

> "I am surely a slave of God. He has given me the Scripture and has made me a prophet. . . . And peace be upon me the day I was born and the day I shall die and the day I shall be raised to [eternal] life." (19:30, 33)

Several *hadith*s of Prophet Muhammad (﷽) refer explicitly to the return of Jesus (﷽) to this earth.

As this world had a beginning, it will also have an end. The period preceding the end will be a time of severe trials and extreme corruption. During that period, God will send His chosen leader, the Guided One (*Mahdi*), who, together with his armies of the righteous, will bring about a reign of justice and peace for a brief period.

After that, the satanic imposter known as the Anti-Christ (*Dajjal*) will make his appearance. This arch-deceiver will confuse and mislead people, luring them to a false, evil religion. Then Jesus (﷽) will return to the earth and kill the Anti-Christ, and a temporary period of goodness and righteousness will follow. Before the cosmic cataclysm which will end the world by God's command, Jesus (﷽), like every created being, will experience death.

Then what is the Islamic belief concerning salvation through Jesus's death and resurrection?

As we've seen, God Himself emphatically states that Jesus (﷽), although a great and honored prophet, was nothing more than a mortal man. God also declares that Jesus (﷽) did not die on the cross but rather was raised up to Him alive.

We have also seen that although Adam and Eve (﷽) sinned, they repented and God immediately forgave them.[31] Since they were freely forgiven by their Lord, there is no burden of collective sin, passed on to the whole human race by our first ancestors, which affects every newborn baby as it comes from its mother's womb, and from which all must be saved. Rather, each human being comes into this life with a pure, wholesome nature and a clean slate. As God proclaims,

> *We surely created the human being in the best of moulds.* (95:4; also 20:50)

For it is our inner state and deeds that bring us near to or take us far from our Lord. Salvation is conferred by God's grace and mercy, not through the sacrifice or vicarious atonement of any intermediary. And each individual's accounting is directly with God.

> *No bearer of burdens can bear another's burden, and if one who is heavily burdened [with sins] calls another to bear his load, he will not be able to bear any of it [for him], even if he is a close relative. . . . And whoever attains purity attains it only for his own soul. And the destination is to God.* (35:18; also 2:286; 6:164; 17:15; 39:7; 53:38)

Since God is endlessly kind, loving, merciful, forgiving and the acceptor of repentance, the notion of Original Sin is a denial of His infinitely beneficent attributes, a negation of His Reality. Without question, the most generous, gracious Lord is able to freely forgive His servants without having to sacrifice the noblest of His creation in order to do so. And the Most Merciful repeatedly assures us that He forgives, out of His end-

less grace and compassion, whomever He wills. No matter what we may have done, His forgiveness is there for
the asking.

> *And seek forgiveness from God. Truly, He is the
> Most Forgiving, the Most Merciful.* (4:106)

> *The one who does evil or wrongs his own soul, and
> then asks God's forgiveness, will find Him Most
> Forgiving, Most Merciful.* (4:110)

> *It is He who accepts repentance and forgives the
> evil [deeds], and He knows whatever you do.* (42:25;
> also 20:82)

MUHAMMAD

In the year 570 CE, Muhammad (ﷺ) was born into
a poor but noble family in Mecca, Arabia. He was a
descendant of the prophet Abraham (ﷺ) through the
line of Ishmael (ﷺ). His father died before he was born
and his mother passed away when he was a young child.
He was then raised by his grandfather for a time. Later,
following his grandfather's death, he was cared for by an
uncle. Like most people of his time, he grew up without
knowing how to read or write.

His people, the Quraish tribe of Mecca, were idol-
worshipers. Although their traditions recognized the
Supreme Deity, they set Him aside as being too remote
to reach. In His place, they worshiped a number of gods.
Since long before Muhammad's time, 360 idols had been
set up inside the Kabah, the sacred House of God built
by Abraham (ﷺ) some 2700 years earlier at his Lord's
command, turning it into a shrine for idol-worship and
pagan pilgrimage.

Meccan society was in a corrupt, decaying state.
There was no centralized government; it was tribe
against tribe, strong against weak, rich against poor,
master against slave. Women could be inherited by their

sons upon the death of their husbands and girl babies were often buried alive. While tribes of Jews and scattered Christians lived in Arabia, neither group propagated its faith. However, the Jews were waiting eagerly for a prophet, whose coming had been foretold in certain sacred texts, to appear from among the House of Jacob (ﷺ). Traditions concerning the coming of a prophet also existed among the Arabian Christians.

THE FIRST REVELATION

Instinctively recognizing God's Oneness and supreme holiness, Muhammad (ﷺ) kept himself away from the idol-worship and depraved practices of his society. He grew into manhood with such a high reputation for honesty that his people referred to him as "the Trustworthy." His character, manners and ways of dealing were so impressive that when he was twenty-five, a wealthy widow named Khadijah, fifteen years his senior, asked if he would marry her. He accepted and she remained his only wife, dearly loved by him and his greatest supporter, until her death twenty-five years later.

By the age of forty, Muhammad (ﷺ) had withdrawn more and more from the company of people, spending much of his time in prayer and meditation. His usual place of retreat was a cave called Hira at the top of a steep, jagged mountain near Mecca.

There, one night, in an indescribably awesome spiritual experience, Muhammad (ﷺ) was visited by a supernatural being. This, although he did not realize it, was the Angel of Revelation, Gabriel (ﷺ). The angel embraced Muhammad (ﷺ) overwhelmingly three successive times, ordering him, "Read!" At this, the confused and frightened Muhammad (ﷺ) three times replied that he did not know how to read. The angel then conveyed to him the first revelation of the Qur'an, saying,

> *Read,*[32] *in the name of your Lord who created—*
> *created the human being from a clot. Read, and your*
> *Lord is the Most Generous, who taught by the pen—*
> *taught the human being what he did not know.* (96:1-5)

And as the vision became more and more intense, the
angel announced to Muhammad (ﷺ) that he was the
Messenger of God.

This, then, was how Muhammad's prophethood
began. For the next twenty-two years, the revelations of
the Qur'an continued to come to him at intervals
through the angel. The early chapters or *surah*s, which
are mostly found toward the end of the Qur'an, deal
largely with the human being's relationship with God,
responsibility and accountability, the certainty of the
coming of the Day of Judgment, and the Life Hereafter.
The language and style of much of this material is
almost stunning in its power of expression and the
impact it has upon the heart and mind of the reader.

MUHAMMAD'S PROPHETHOOD

At first Muhammad (ﷺ) was deeply alarmed and
troubled by his overwhelming experience in the cave.
Without any knowledge of earlier revealed religions or
scriptures, he had no context in which to understand its
meaning. But soon the angel returned with further revelations. Gradually Muhammad's role as messenger and
prophet became clear to him.

Presently, at God's command, he began to speak to
those closest to him about what he had received. Their
response was immediately to accept his way, thus
becoming the first Muslims. Later, God ordered
Muhammad (ﷺ) to call the people of his corrupt society
to repent, abandon idolatry, and submit to and worship
Him alone. But his Message was at once perceived as a
threat by the pagan leaders, an obvious challenge to

their power and authority. Consequently, Muhammad's preaching was met with intense hostility by the powerful among his people. Only a small number of individuals grasped the truth of the Message and accepted the guidance.

At first, Muhammad (ﷺ) was ridiculed and opposed by the pagan leader of the Quraish. Then, one by one, they began to employ other tactics: insults, bribery, threats, defamation, harassment, physical abuse, boycott, and ultimately an attempt at assassination. At the same time, the lowly and helpless among his followers were severely persecuted. The pagans were so threatened by the religion of moral responsibility, righteousness, justice and equality which the formerly trusted Muhammad (ﷺ) was preaching that they used every possible means to force him to give up his mission, and also to force the Muslims to abandon Islam.

But the Prophet (ﷺ) and the Muslims remained steadfast and patient. No threat of any kind could keep them from holding firmly to the truth once it had become clear to them. Several of the first Muslims were cruelly tortured and a few died as martyrs to their faith. To escape persecution, others emigrated to Abyssinia (Ethiopia), a neighboring country ruled by a devout Christian king who secretly accepted Islam. And at God's command, the Prophet (ﷺ) continued steadfastly to preach His Message.

Still, all his efforts were met with rejection. When he went to Taif, a nearby town, its people not only refused to listen to him, but street urchins pelted him with stones until the blood ran. Then, in the tenth year of the his mission, a handful of people came to Mecca from Yathrib, another city in western Arabia. They heard about the Prophet's preaching, met with him in secret, and were deeply impressed.

After accepting Islam at Muhammad's hand, these new Muslims returned home to Yathrib to teach the faith to their fellow citizens. Within two years, their number had increased greatly. Again, a number of the Muslims of Yathrib met secretly with the Prophet (ﷺ) in Mecca. At that time, they begged him to come to their city and be their leader, pledging to support him with their lives if necessary. And the Messenger of God (ﷺ) promised to accept their invitation.

THE MIGRATION (HIJRAH)

The persecuted Muslims of Mecca left secretly for Yathrib in small groups. As discretely as possible, they made their way across the desert to the town whose Muslims had opened their hearts to them.

Then, at God's command, the Prophet (ﷺ) prepared to leave Mecca. One night, when almost all the Muslims had left, a group of pagans armed with swords surrounded his house to assassinate him. But God's Messenger (ﷺ) slipped out unseen among his would-be attackers and left the city with his closest friend, Abu Bakr. God saved the two from the intensive manhunt of the pagans which followed, and they reached Yathrib, about three hundred miles distant, after several days of travel.

The Messenger of God (ﷺ) was welcomed to his new home by crowds of enthusiastic Muslims of Yathrib. The city was soon renamed Medinat an-Nabi, the City of the Prophet. We know it today simply as Medina.

THE ISLAMIC COMMUNITY IN MEDINA

At last the Prophet (ﷺ) was away from the day-to-day persecutions of the pagans. Now, established in his new city as its leader, he was able to give form to the system and the community God had commanded him to establish.

It was during the period in Medina that the various sections of the Qur'an containing the rules of Islam were revealed. Whenever a new command from God was transmitted to the Prophet (☶) by the angel Gabriel (☶), it was put into practice by the Muslims as soon as they heard the verses from the Prophet's lips. And now, in addition to laws and injunctions relating to worship and human interaction, God addressed the social, economic and international affairs of the Muslim community (*ummah*).

However, even in Medina there was no peace for the Messenger of God (☶) and his community, for they were now repeatedly harassed by the threats and military expeditions of the Meccan pagans. Within Medina itself, there were also hostile groups ready to side with and assist the enemy. Several major battles and military campaigns followed. Although few in number and ill-equipped for battle, the Muslims fought with great courage, empowered by their faith.

With God's help, within ten years, the Prophet (☶) and the believers had won various decisive military and diplomatic victories over their enemies. God's Messenger (☶) then entered the city of Mecca, from which he had fled several years earlier under threat of his life, as the spiritual and temporal leader of its people, who accepted Islam as a body.

Instead of reproaching or taking revenge upon those who had persecuted him so cruelly, he forgave even his most bitter enemies. Thus, the "opening" of Mecca took place peacefully. The Prophet (☶) then entered the Kabah and with his own hands destroyed all the idols which had been placed there by the pagans. Once again the sacred House was purified for the worship of God, the Praised and Exalted, alone. And soon afterwards, God sent down the final revelation of the Qur'an:

> *This day I have perfected your religion for you and*
> *completed My favor upon you, and have chosen for you*
> *Islam as your religion.* (5:3/5:4 in some translations)

The Sunnah *and* Hadith

The Prophet, may God's infinite peace and blessings be upon him, left this world for the Eternal Home less than three months later. He had delivered the sacred Message which God had entrusted to him with total faithfulness. And he left behind, for all time to come, two permanent, unchangeable sources of guidance for mankind: the Holy Qur'an and the record of his own example and practice, which is known as the *sunnah*.[33]

God refers to Muhammad ( ) in the Qur'an as "*the Seal of the Prophets*" (33:40)—that is, as the last prophet and messenger, who set a seal of finality upon the prophetic line. This means that there can be no prophets whomsoever after him.

Now, why should this be so? The answer is simple. Since the Qur'an contains God's final, complete guidance for all mankind up to the end of this world, it does not need any amendment, restatement or change. Besides this, the Messenger of God ( ) was much more than merely a conveyer of his Lord's guidance. He was also the flawless example of how it is to be lived—the perfect human being, God's beloved (*habeeb*). God says concerning His Last Prophet ( ),

> *You surely have in the Messenger of God a beautiful example for the one who hopes in God and the Last Day, and remembers God much.* (33:21)

God also refers to Muhammad ( ) as "*a mercy for all mankind*" (21:107) and as "*a witness and a bringer of good news and a warner, and a caller to God, by His leave, and a lamp giving light*" (33:45-46; also 35:23-24). "*Truly, God and His angels bless the Prophet,*" He declares, ordering, "*O you who believe, invoke blessings upon the Prophet and greet him with a goodly greeting*" (33:56). As his wife Aisha said about him, "His nature was the Qur'an." And up to this day, Muslims throughout the world try to pattern their lives upon his, regarding the Noblest of Mankind (ﷺ) as the best example to be followed in all matters, both great and small.

In the years following the Prophet's death, the details of his *sunnah* were collected, verified and classified by a number of extraordinarily God-fearing, painstaking scholars. These men worked according to the highest standards of truthfulness and accuracy, fearing the dire punishment of falsifying anything concerning the Messenger of God (ﷺ). They compiled vast numbers of well-documented verbal reports known as *hadith*s, transmitted by the first generation of Muslims and mostly going back to the Prophet (ﷺ) himself.

The collections of *hadith* contain reports of the Prophet's actions, sayings, and what he approved or disapproved of in others. These reports cover an immensely wide range of subjects, from the most public to the most personal. Probably more details have been preserved concerning the Prophet's actions and words than any other person's, including the best-known of present-day figures.

After the Prophet's death, Islam spread very rapidly to various parts of the world. It was carried by men whose lives and societies had been transformed by the certainty of their faith. At its height (700-1600 CE), the Islamic empire extended from Spain to the Philippines. During the period when European civilization was still in a quite primitive state, religion, culture, government, architecture, art and science flourished widely in Muslim lands as a result of impetus provided by Islam.

4 THE HEREAFTER—THE DAY OF JUDGMENT, HEAVEN AND HELL

Belief in the existence of a life after this life is the fifth article of faith in Islam. Belief in the Hereafter is so essential that it has been mentioned again and again in the Qur'an as complementary to belief in God. And understanding why this is so is extremely important.

The existence of a future life is a spiritual reality which we are able to know about with certainty only through divine revelation. Because our ultimate destiny lies with that future life and not with this temporary life, it is only just and right that we should be informed about it and thus be able to work for it, for it pertains to our reality as humans. God says,

> O you human creature, you are toiling toward your Lord with a [difficult] toil and you shall meet Him. (84:6)

The Prophet (ﷺ) advised believers to think of death often. Devout Muslims certainly do so, regarding it as the door which connects one state of existence to another. And surely most of us have, at some point, wondered, "What will the end be like for me? Will it be painful? Exactly what is going to happen? And does something come after it or not?"

These are extremely critical questions which we should ask, not in order to be morbid but so that we can prepare ourselves for the most important experience we have yet to undergo. Death is not something we can conveniently put aside as relating to the far future. None of us knows when it will come to us, and when it does come, it will be too late to do anything. Therefore, it's important for us to feel at home with the subject, regarding death not as the final ending of our existence but as the opening of our return to our Lord. And it's something whose favorable outcome we need to strive for throughout the whole of our conscious life. For it is at death that our efforts of a lifetime become all-important as the goods we trade in for an eternal existence of happiness or misery.

It is a fact we human beings generally seek out what we enjoy and try to avoid what we don't—that is, unless we have a strong motivation to do otherwise. Certainly, to act purely for the sake of God is the highest form of motivation. But most of us just aren't that noble and unselfish. Our human nature is such that, without the promise of reward or fear of punishment, very few of us would act as God wants us to. We need some incentive to cause us to act according to our higher selves. And the desire for Paradise and fear of Hell is precisely such a strong motivation.

The Materialist Versus the Spiritual Point of View

In every society, at every time, people who believe only in this temporary material life have argued against the existence of an afterlife. Many have used such arguments as an excuse for doing whatever they like. The Qur'an is full of references to such people.

> *And they say, "When we are bones and fragments, shall we really be resurrected again as a new creation?" Say, [O Muhammad:] "[Yes,] even if you are stones or iron, or a created thing that is even greater than that in your estimation." They will say, "Who will bring us back to life?" Say: "The One who created you the first time." Then they will shake their heads at you and say, "When will it be?" Say: "Perhaps it is near."* (17:49-51; also 17:98; 19:66-67; 34:7; 36:78-79; 37:15-17)

> *Those who disbelieve imagine that they will not be raised again. Say, [O Muhammad:] "On the contrary, by my Lord! You shall be raised again, and then you will be informed of what you did. And that is easy for my Lord."* (64:7)

The arguments of such people have no basis in logic,

for God, who creates and destroys, can just as easily re-create. He can also change the attributes and forms of His creation as He wills—as, for example, water changes from a liquid to a solid or a gas. In the same fashion, a body can cease to possess the characteristics of life and apparently become a piece of inert matter. But there is no proof whatsoever that this finishes the existence of the occupant of that body, the soul.

The collective spiritual experience of mankind attests to the fact that the former 'tenant' has now vacat-ed its former home and gone somewhere else—or, to put it in different terms, has been transformed into another form of energy. Therefore, God's supremely logical answer to the materialists' question, *"When I am dead, shall I really be brought forth alive?"* is, *"Does not the human being remember that We created him before, when he was nothing?"* (19:66-67).

THE LAST DAY, THE RESURRECTION
AND THE JUDGMENT

In many verses of the Qur'an such as the above, God, who knows everything there is to know about His cre-ation, denies the claim of the materialists that death constitutes the final, absolute end of our existence. For our perishable, material bodies, it does, of course, but for our immortal souls, this present life is only one brief stage on its journey from God to God. And our Lord informs us repeatedly that our temporary life on this earth is merely a trial, a test, an examination period. For what? To prepare ourselves for the future life of endless duration.

In this life, each hour, each day, we are faced with individual tests whose combined results will determine our future happiness or suffering. For each of us, death will mark the ending of our personal exam. It will be fol-lowed by the Day of Resurrection and Judgment, whose coming is as certain as the fact that we are alive.

> *Be mindful of a Day on which you will return to God. Then each soul will be recompensed for whatever it earned, and they shall not be wronged.* (2:281; also 2:48, 123; 3:9-10, 25, 185; 4:87; 6:12; 10:45, 11:08, 103; 16:111 and dozens of other verses)

No one except God knows when that Day will come. But what is certain is that, as the universe had a beginning, it will also have an end.

> *The analogy of the life of this world is only like water. We send it down from the sky and then mingle it with the produce of the earth, from which people and cattle eat; until, when the earth has put on its ornaments and is embellished, and its people think that they have all power over it, Our command reaches it by night or by day, whereupon We cause it to be utterly destroyed, as if it had not flourished the previous day. Thus do We explain the signs for people who reflect.* (10:24)

This end will take place in a manner frightful beyond imagination, and at that time every living thing on earth will die.

> *When the Trumpet will be blown with a single blowing, and the earth and the mountains will be lifted up and crushed with a single crushing — then, on that Day, the Event will befall; and the sky will be split apart, for on that Day it will be torn, and the angels will be on its sides; and on that Day eight angels will carry the Throne of your Lord above them. That Day on which you will be brought to judgment, not a secret of yours will be hidden.* (69:13-18)

> *When the sky is shattered and when the seas are poured forth and when the graves are overturned, a*

soul will know what it sent on ahead and what it left behind. (82:1-5; also 81:1-14)

At that time, the dead will be raised and their newly-recreated bodies will be rejoined with their souls. And the Judgment will take place.

Each of us will be shown the book of our life's deeds, recorded by our two companion angels. None of us will be able to deny the truthfulness of the record or to make any excuses. The record will be final, closed and unchangeable, and we will be judged accordingly, as our good and bad deeds are weighed against each other in a perfectly just scale.

> *The weighing that Day will be true. Then those whose scale [of goodness] is heavy, they will be the successful, and those whose scale is light, they will be the ones who will have lost their souls because they acted wrongly with regard to Our revelations.* (7:8-9)

> *We have tied each person's destiny to his neck, and on the Day of Resurrection We shall bring forth for him a book which he will find wide open, [saying,] "Read your book! This Day your soul is sufficient as an accountant against yourself."* (17:13-14)

> *And whoever does an atom's weight of good shall see it, and whoever does an atom's weight of evil shall see it.* (99:7-8)

The verses of the Qur'an dealing with these matters are extremely numerous. Their tone is dead earnest, conveying total certainty. The effect of their message, stated and restated again and again, is to produce a conviction in the heart of the listener/reader of the absolute truth of what is being said. For example:

> *The Day on which the sky will become like molten*

copper and the mountains will become like shreds of wool, and no close friend will ask of a friend, although they will see one another—the guilty one will long to ransom himself from the punishment   of that Day through his children and his spouse and his brother and his relatives who sheltered him. By no means! It is the fire of Hell, plucking away to the skull, calling to those who turn their backs [on the truth] and turn away [from goodness], and collect and withhold [their wealth from doing good with it]. (70:8-18)

The Day when the Trumpet is blown, whosoever is in the heavens and whosoever is on the earth will be terrified, excepting the one whom God wills. And all will come to Him humble. . . . Whoever brings a good deed, he will have better than it, and whoever brings an evil deed, they will be thrown down on their faces in the Fire. Are you recompensed with anything other than what you did? (27:87, 89-90; also 17:97)

O mankind, be mindful of God and fear a Day when no father will make the least compensation for his son, nor will any son make compensation for his father. God's promise is surely true. Then do not let the life of this world deceive you, nor let the Deceiver [Satan] deceive you concerning God. (31:33)

GOD'S INFINITE MERCY
AND ABSOLUTE JUSTICE

God is the Most Just Judge. At the same time, He is the Most Compassionate and the Most Merciful. *"Your Lord has ordained mercy upon Himself"* (6:54), He assures us, declaring through His Prophet (ﷺ) that His mercy overcomes His anger.[34] He also commands us, His servants, not to despair of His mercy, saying,

O My servants who have committed excesses against yourselves, do not despair of the mercy of God.

*Truly, God forgives all sins. He is surely the Most
Forgiving, the Most Merciful.* (39:53)

*And who despairs of the mercy of his Lord except
those who are astray?* (15:56)

Therefore, our hearts should find comfort in knowing
that no matter what sins we may have committed, our
infinitely gracious Lord is able and willing to forgive
them all if we turn to Him. For He knows every single
thing about us: the frailty of our human nature, our
physical and emotional makeup, the conditions under
which we live, the difficulties surrounding us and our
capacity to deal with them, the pressures and tempta-
tions we are subject to, the most subtle whispers of our
hearts. And He assures us that

*We do not burden any soul beyond its capacity, and
with Us is a record which speaks with truth, and they
shall not be wronged.* (23:62)

Moreover, out of His mercy, God sends us, by day and
by night, repeated opportunities to do good (and refrain-
ing from doing a possible evil is also a form of good). No
matter how small a deed may be in our eyes, in God's
sight it may be important and a means of forgiveness or
reward for us, as if He were just searching for reasons to
show us mercy.[35]

In addition to all this, our Lord grants us still another divine mercy: that He judges our actions by our *intentions*—that is, by what we intend in our hearts rather
than by what we actually do. The Prophet (ﷺ) stated
that if someone intends to do a good deed but does not
carry it out, God writes one good deed for him. If he
intends to do a good deed and actually carries it out, God
writes for him a reward of between ten to seven hundred
times, to many more than that. However, if someone

intends to do a bad deed but does not carry it out, God writes one good deed for him, whereas if he intends to do a bad deed and actually carries it out, God writes only a single bad deed in his account.[36]

> *The one who brings a good deed, for him there will be [a reward of] tenfold like it, while the one who brings an evil deed will be recompensed only with the like of it, and they will not be treated unjustly.* (6:160)

But still it must also be known that, in spite of our Lord's infinite mercy, there is punishment for those people who persistently deny and rebel against their Creator, reject His guidance, produce evil and harm others, in spite of all the opportunities sent to them for reflection and doing good. As a requirement of God's perfect justice, such punishment *must be*: workers must be paid for their work, whether good or evil, and the workers of good and evil cannot be paid the same.

> *Is the one who keeps in mind God's pleasure like the one who has earned God's condemnation and whose abode is the Fire?—and how evil a journey's end!* (3:162)

For the deniers of God and workers of evil, their place will be Hell, for as long as their Lord decrees. In that unimaginable horrible place, their companions will be others who, like themselves, were completely alienated from Him. They will have endless regrets about the wasting of their lives and the harm they did, and will suffer enduring torment and agony in proportion to the evil of their deeds. The picture which God paints of their future life is truly a frightful one.

> *And if you could only see how, when those who disbelieve die, the angels strike their faces and their*

> *backs, [saying,] "Then taste the punishment of the burning! That is for what your hands have sent ahead, for truly, God is not unjust to His servants." (8:50-51)*

> *And those who earned evil, their recompense will be an evil like it, and darkness will cover them. They will have no protector from God, as if their faces were overshadowed by pieces of the darkness of night. Those are the people of the Fire; they will remain in it. (10:27)*

But while Hell is the place of recompense for evil, it is at the same time the place for cleaning. Throughout our lives, our compassionate Lord sends us opportunities, in the form of troubles and suffering, to be cleansed from the evil of our inner state and deeds. If this cleansing is not sufficient, after we leave this life Hell is the domain in which our cleaning is finally completed. And according to the flawless divine justice, when it is finished, many souls will be taken out of Hell and admitted to Paradise and the Divine Presence of their Lord. For if there is any trace of faith or goodness in the heart of a servant of His, He will not permit it to be lost.

> *Assuredly God does not do even an atom's weight of injustice, and if there is a good deed, He will double it and will give [the doer of it], from His Presence, a great reward. (4:40)*

This is made clear by certain *hadiths* of the Prophet (صلى الله عليه وسلم),[37] to whom God will give the power of intercession and permission to take souls out of Hellfire.

Then, also in keeping with God's perfect justice, those who believed in their Lord, obeyed His guidance, and tried to please Him, will have an eternal reward for their goodness. *"The people of Paradise will have, on that Day, the best abode and the most beautiful place of rest"* (25:24), God promises. Moreover, *"No soul knows what delights are hidden from them, as a reward for what they used to do"* (32:17). Those surrendered, obedient servants will have everything their hearts could desire, surrounded by pure and noble companions and scenes, in the Presence of their beloved Lord, for whose pleasure they lived their lives.

> *And those who believed and did righteous deeds—no soul do We burden beyond its capacity — those are the people of Paradise; they will remain in it. And We shall remove any ill feeling from their hearts, rivers flowing beneath them. And they will say, "All praise be to God who guided us to this, for if God has not guided us, we could not have been guided. The messengers of God surely brought the truth." And it will be called out [to them,] "This is Paradise! You have inherited it because of what you used to do."* (7:42-43)

Because of this understanding, conscious Muslims actually live in two worlds: the present world and the world-to-come. For we know that our task is to strive in this life to the best of our abilities with whatever God has given us, whether it is much or little. In every situation, we try to consider whether a thing is good for our future life, as well as for the present. More than anything, we fear our Lord's anger and displeasure; above all else, we desire His pleasure and love.

This serves as our primary motivation when faced with a choice between good and evil possibilities. It is the force that enables us to control our passions and desires, exchanging temporary satisfactions in this brief life for permanent happiness in the Eternal Life; for we know that

> *Whatever has been given to you is only a convenience of this life, and what is with God is better and more lasting for those who believe and trust in their Lord.* (42:36)

The message of all this is therefore one of hope and

trust: hope in our Lord's endless, all-embracing compassion and mercy, and trust that He will accept us, forgive us and deal gently with us, out of His infinite grace.

6 THE DIVINE DECREE

While this is the last of Islam's articles of faith, it is of the greatest importance for our lives. It can be summed up in one brief, comprehensive sentence: "All things, both good and evil, proceed from God Most High."

But what does this actually mean? In summary, this statement tells us that all things proceed from a single, unified Will and Command—God's. Nothing is outside it; as God is One, so all things are part of a great, integrated whole that proceeds from His Oneness. Good is part of His plan and so is evil—or what seems evil to our limited perspective. Consequently, whatever happens has been permitted and decreed by God; conversely, if something does not happen, it is because He did not permit or decree it. Thus, He instructs His beloved Prophet (ﷺ) to say,

> *Nothing can happen to us except what God has decreed for us. He is our Protector, and let the believers put their trust in God.* (9:51)

UNDERSTANDING SUFFERING AND EVIL

This matter poses an extremely difficult problem for a great many people. On the one hand, God asks us to believe that He is infinitely loving, perfectly just, and endlessly merciful and compassionate. But at the same time, He permits evil to thrive and the most horrible things to happen, often to the most innocent or best people. How are we to make sense out of this?

We've all heard of people who questioned or lost their faith when faced with severe difficulties or calamities—for themselves, their loved ones, their nation. At such a time, one may feel that if God were really there and cared, He would not have allowed such awful things to happen or evil to flourish unchecked. The obvious conclusion to be drawn from such a line of reasoning is either that God does not exist or, if He does, He is completely indifferent to human suffering.

If we put ourselves into the mind of a person who has just passed through some horrendous personal calamity, his thinking might be something like the following:

"Where was God while all this was happening to me, and how could He have let it happen? And why me— what did *I* do to deserve it? I'm not a really bad person, so why would God do this to me?" And he feels let down, betrayed. "God should have done something to stop this catastrophe," he thinks. The trust he formerly felt in the goodness, stability and predictability of life—of God Himself—has been shattered. Even if at some later time things return to normal, or even to a state of high happiness, the fear and uncertainty may continue to haunt him.

Hence, when calamities come, people who think like this either lose their faith or become so angry and bitter toward God that they stop having any dealings with Him. Such a surge of doubt and despair within the heart of a person who is going through a difficult test is documented in several verses of the Qur'an, such as the following:

> *The human being does not tire of praying for good,*
> *and if evil touches him, he is despairing, hopeless.*
> (41:49; also 11:9-11; 17:83; 30:36-37)

But such attitudes are based on an incorrect understanding of things. God is not our servant or nursemaid, to give us whatever we want whenever we ask for it. He is God, the All-Knowing, All-Wise, All-Powerful

Controller of all things in existence, who is aware of the minutest parts of His creation as well as the whole. His attributes, His Will and His divine plan are perfect. And the individual destiny of each one of us is inseparably connected to and interwoven with the whole of this immense cosmic plan.

What we must realize is that God's existence and His perfect attributes do not depend on anything that happens or does not happen to any part of His creation. For example, if everything suddenly ceased to exist except God Himself, would God have changed as a result? Obviously not, for He is God, the masterless Master of all creation.

Consequently, created things can never be taken as the measure or criterion of God and His workings. No matter what calamities may occur in some parts of the earth or to individual people, God remains as He always was, and He will continue to be so for all eternity. Despite suffering and evil on the earth, His endless glory and greatness continue to be manifested throughout His creation: the sun, moon and stars keep to their appointed orbits, the mountains stand firm in their places, the waves of the oceans continue on their endless, rolling course; birds still fly, flowers go on blooming, and each human soul moves toward its final destiny.

From this, it becomes clear that the two negative 'conclusions' mentioned above—that either God does not exist or, if He does, He is indifferent to human pain—are incorrect. The existence of creation proves that a Creator must exist. And His answers to prayers, His ever-present help and support to His servants, demonstrates that He is always with us and is not indifferent to anything which affects us. Indeed, He reaches out to us and gently calls us back to Himself, saying,

O you human creature, what has made you heed-

less of your Lord, the Most Generous, who created you,
then fashioned you, then proportioned you? (82:6-7)

But we must accept the fact that God created a universe which operates according to established laws, both physical and spiritual—laws which take effect regardless of who is involved. If, in the operation of these laws, something happens that hurts one of His servants, it does not negate God's existence, power or His infinite goodness in the least.

As for the existence of evil, it is an integral part of the divine plan. The All-Wise, All-Knowing Lord made Satan as a test for His servants, permitting him to carry on his mischievous activities without hindrance. And while God has promised that Satan will never be given power over His sincere, obedient servants,[38] a great many people—perhaps today more than ever—respond to his call. Using their freedom of choice, they choose evil and thereby become workers for Satan's cause, in contrast to the firm, committed workers for God, who steadfastly refuse to cooperate with and become part of evil in any form. But even though God may permit those who choose evil to flourish for a while, the divine judgment and punishment *must* fall upon them as a result, either in this life or in the Hereafter, or both.

The problem for us, when faced with calamities, lies in the fact that we know that it is God who permitted our suffering. Consequently, if we allow bitterness and resentment to rule our inner state, we often end up blaming Him for our troubles. At the same time, in our helplessness, we're obliged to recognize that, as He brought our affliction upon us, He is the only One who can remove it. Moreover, He is also the One who helps, supports and comforts us throughout it. Therefore, it is essential to always keep one thing in mind in the midst of a crisis: that only God knows the ultimate destiny of each part of His creation and that His plan for it—including ourselves—is perfect, while we know only our immediate situation.

Therefore, coming to terms with reality requires that we recognize, first, that God Almighty is the sole arranger of our lives; second, that life is made up of tests; and third, that every test is arranged by divine wisdom.

THE DIVINE WISDOM OF TESTS AND TRIALS

Understanding and accepting that tests and trials are going to come, *must* come to all, is the first step in reconciliation with God if some calamity has alienated us from Him. *"We shall surely test you"* (2:155), our Lord declares. But it's also important to understand that tests consist not only of suffering and difficulties. In actuality, they consist of everything in our lives. Tests lie hidden even in what is most dear to us—our spouses, our children, our possessions.[39] And each test is different and tailored uniquely to ourselves. As God says,

> *It is He who has made you stewards on the earth and has raised some of you in ranks above others, in order to test you in what He has given you.* (6:165)

The river of humanity continues to run toward its Lord, and as it runs, tests run with it—alternating tests of hardship and tests of ease. If God gives us good health, power, status, wealth, peace, happiness and pleasure, we're tested just as much by our good circumstances as the suffering person is tested by his misfortunes, misery, losses and deep inner agony. And our Lord is looking to see what we do with His manifold favors or with the searing pain that He sends us. This is the meaning of His words,

> *If a wound has touched you, [other] people have*
> *been touched by a wound like it, for such are the days*
> *[of varying fortunes] which We alternate among*
> *mankind. . . . Or do you suppose that you will enter*
> *Paradise while God does not know those among you*
> *who strive or know the patient?* (3:140, 142; also 2:214)

Why God sends us a particular test (whether it happens to consist of inheriting ten million dollars or losing everything we have; of possessing radiant health or being struck down by a critical illness; of building a stately mansion or having our home leveled by a hurricane; of seeing a loved one live to a ripe old age or become the early victim of violence), we cannot know. Nonetheless, our trust in God gives us the certainty that this test must be useful and beneficial for us in some way or the other.

Islam teaches us that tests serve very important purposes. The first is to remove from us the burden of some of our sins, the filth which has accumulated on our hearts during this life. For none of us can enter Paradise and come into the Divine Presence with the dirt of this life upon us; in order to come to our Lord, we must be clean. And God informs us through His blessed Prophet (ﷺ) that any suffering we experience serves as a means of cleansing us of our sins.[40]

The second purpose of tests is to give us high ranks in the life-to-come, ranks that we could never attain through a life without troubles. So, while Muslims suffer pain and hurt just as much as anyone else, we possess the certainty that everything God sends us has a beneficial purpose and outcome, both for cleaning us and for raising our ranks.[41]

Another point must not be overlooked. The same situation which is a test for the one who is experiencing it is often a test for those close to him or her. For example, the parents of a child dying of cancer may suffer as much or more than the child itself. Many of us who witness and work with the victims of calamities share their sufferings, so that the sufferers' pain is part of *our* test, too. Hence, the same criteria can be applied to those who share in tests as to the immediate individual who is tested.

Being successful in passing tests requires two things: unending patience and deep, unwavering trust in God. When difficulties come, anger, resentment, bitterness and complaints can only add to our problems. What helps is surrendering instead of fighting, and exercising firmness, patience, steadfastness and self-control. What brings consolation is remembering and crying out to the very One who sent us this difficulty—who is also the only One who is able to take it away. *"Then flee to God"* (51:50), our Lord advises, for *"There is no refuge from God except in Him"* (9:118).

Because our vision is limited, we're seldom able to see the divine wisdom in a calamity at the time it strikes us or those we love, whose tests we share. But perhaps years later, we may be able to realize the good that it brought us, terrible though it seemed at the time. For sometimes we have to pass through a very narrow passageway in order to reach a broader, more spacious territory. At the very least, on the Day of Judgment, we will come to know the blessing of that calamity, as it took away from us the burden of many of our sins and raised us to a high rank in the Divine Presence.

PUTTING IT ALL INTO PERSPECTIVE

Since God's Will is over our own personal wills, it is a permanent, unchangeable reality that He can do with us whatever He sees fit. But because most of us do not trust in His Will, we scramble around, desperately trying to control and manage our own destinies with whatever resources we have at our disposal. We're convinced that we know what's best for ourselves and can do it better than anyone else—especially God, the mysterious, hidden, unseen Being, who may spring unwanted 'surprises' on us.

So we do whatever seems right to us at the time, sometimes getting our way and achieving our goals, and at other times making this, that or the other mistake with our lives. Rarely are we sufficiently surrendered to trust God's choices for us to be correct rather than our own, often wrong ones. Only when we recognize and accept our Lord's divine Will as being above and superior to our own do we feel secure in the knowledge that He will lead us to the best possible outcome and destiny.

Islam is often accused of encouraging fatalism or passiveness. But this is due to an incorrect understanding. Passiveness is not part of the Islamic way; rather, acceptance and surrender are. From our side, we must take whatever positive action we can to deal with problems and help ourselves. Nevertheless, when our Lord decrees that our path takes us through troubles, sufferings or evil, including the worst imaginable scenarios, we have confidence that the ultimate outcome will be good, either during this life or in the Hereafter, and hopefully in both. For our Lord is the Trustworthy One (*al-Ameen*), and He will not betray our trust in Him. Instead, He will reward it and bring us through our test in safety. In short, we have trust in Him *as our Lord* to do what is best for us. "If this is what He wants for me," we may say, "I accept it and will try to be patient," according to His words,

> *By Time, truly the human being is in [a state of] loss, excepting those who believe and do righteous deeds, and counsel one another of truth and counsel one another of patience.* (103:1-3)

In the following verse of His all-wise Qur'an, God

concisely summarizes for us the true meaning of the Divine Decree, declaring that

> *No calamity befalls on the earth or within your-*
> *selves without its being in a Book [of decrees] before We*
> *bring it into existence. That is surely easy for God, in*
> *order that you may not grieve over what has passed you*
> *by nor exult over what has been given to you.* (57:22-23)

This understanding is endlessly reassuring. Due to it, even under the most difficult tests, the convinced Muslim's trust and reliance upon God rarely falls apart, and prohibited 'props' such as alcohol or drugs, or the awful sin of taking one's own life, are seldom resorted to. Rather, Muslims use prayer, reading the Qur'an, and the remembrance of God (*dhikr-Allah*) as their primary solace and source of strength, as our Lord advises:

> *O you who believe, seek help with patience and*
> *prayer [salat]. Surely God is with the patient. . . . And*
> *We shall certainly test you with something of fear and*
> *hunger and loss of wealth and lives and fruits. But*
> *give good news to the patient—those who, when a*
> *calamity strikes them, say, "Surely we belong to God*
> *and to Him we shall return."*[42] *Those are the ones upon*
> *whom are blessings from their Lord and mercy, and*
> *those are the rightly-guided.* (2:153-157)

Belief in the Divine Decree is therefore a statement of confidence in God's infinite wisdom and knowledge, and the absolute perfection and purposefulness of His divine plan. It is not fatalism, passiveness or resignation; rather, it is the essential component of a Muslim's trust, reliance upon and submission to God's Will as it manifests itself. Put another way, it is an understanding that, regardless of what human beings may will, God's

Will is the one which must prevail, and a willingness to trust in and surrender to that Will because it cannot be anything other than good.

> *And whoever is mindful of God, He will make a way out [of his difficulties] for him and will provide for him from [sources] which he could not imagine. And whoever trusts in God, He will be sufficient for Him.* (65:2-3)

IV
THE ACTS OF WORSHIP

After learning about the Islamic beliefs, it can logically be asked, Just how do Muslims always keep them in mind and live by them? And the answer is, firstly, through the acts of worship prescribed by God.

However, we've seen that God doesn't need anything from any of His creation, and He certainly doesn't need our worship, praise or glorification. We worship Him because, as our Lord, He is entitled to our worship, which is the sign of our submission, obedience and love for Him. And *we* are the ones who benefit by our worship, because it keeps our relationship with Him alive, clear and strong.

God has ordered Muslims to worship Him by means of the following prescribed acts:

1. making the Declaration of Faith (*Shahadah*);
2. observing the five daily prayers (*salat*);
3. fasting during the month of Ramadan (*sawm*);
4. giving the poor-due (*zakat*);
5. performing the pilgrimage to Mecca (*hajj*).

These worships are practiced just as the Prophet (ﷺ) used to practice them. For example, we pray as the Messenger of God (ﷺ) prayed, and his teacher for the prayer (*salat*) was the angel Gabriel (﷽). We fast as the Prophet (﷽) fasted, following the rules he laid down. We perform the pilgrimage (*hajj*) as he performed it, and he performed it as the prophet Abraham (﷽) performed it thousands of years earlier, also taught by the angel Gabriel (﷽). In everything, the Prophet (﷽), the noblest and most perfect of mankind, is our model and example, which we feel proud and honored to follow.

1 THE DECLARATION OF FAITH (*SHAHADAH*)

The first and primary act of worship is to testify to our faith with the declaration, "I bear witness that there is no deity except God, and I bear witness that Muhammad is the Messenger of God—in Arabic, "*Ashhadu an la ilaha illa-Llah, wa ashhadu anna Muhammadu Rasool-Allah.*"

"There is no deity except God"—if this seems too obvious to mention, we really shouldn't have too much trouble in identifying all the little 'gods' which people give their devotion to. It's hardly possible to argue this point, for we human beings, especially in this super-materialistic age, are devoted to so many gods that there's really no end to them.

However, if there *is* no deity except God, it follows that no one else can possibly be worthy of our worship. Our service, obedience and devotion are the right of our Creator alone. Therefore, the first part of the Declaration of Faith is a statement of two things: our belief in God's Oneness, and His sole, unconditional right to be acknowledged as the Lord.

In the second part of the Declaration, we're witnessing to and affirming the fact that Muhammad (﷽) is God's Messenger, proclaiming that we believe in his messengership and prophethood, and that we accept the Message which he brought as coming from our Creator.

We are thereby also proclaiming our intention to follow the guidance that he brought from his Lord and his noble life-example or *sunnah*.

2 THE FIVE DAILY PRAYERS (*SALAT*)

Salat, the obligatory Islamic prayer, is the most stressed and important worship in Islam. But *salat* is not a 'prayer' in the usual sense of the word. Rather, it is a brief worship service, observed five times a day, for the remembrance and glorification of God Most High. During this worship, we stand and recite passages from the Holy Qur'an, and glorify and praise God as we bow, prostrate and kneel before Him.

The times of the five prayers correspond to the various periods of activity of the day. We begin our day with *salat* at dawn, the time when the world is awakening from the night's sleep. Noontime, when we've finished with the morning's activities and generally take a break for lunch or a seista,[43] is the time of the second *salat*. The third *salat* is observed in the latter part of the afternoon, at around the time when people return home from work for the day (or, as is the case in some parts of the world, when they return to work following the afternoon break). Sunset, when the day's activities are finished and night is approaching, is the time of the fourth *salat*. The fifth is observed during the night.

It should be noted that the timing of each *salat* is not a fixed moment, such as 12:33 or 6:05. Instead, the timings all cover a span of time—for example, from 6:05 to 7:20 a.m. or from 12:33 to 2:45 p.m. Although it's most excellent to pray early in the time period, we can pray at any time during it.

In Muslim countries, the call to prayer (*adhan*) from mosques informs worshipers that the time of a prayer has begun and that the congregational *salat* will shortly be observed in the mosque. In the Western world, most

mosques or Islamic centers furnish local prayer schedules so that it's easy to keep up with the *salat* timings.

WHY PRAYER FIVE TIMES A DAY?

What does observing *salat* this often do for Muslims?
The answer is, it keeps us connected to God and helps us
to maintain a close relationship with Him. It reminds of
His guidance, our responsibilities, and the future meeting with Him in the Hereafter. Regular *salat* also helps
us keep away from evil and temptation, fosters strong
personal discipline, and assists in the cleaning of our
hearts, as God advises:

> *Seek help in patience and prayer, although that is
> surely difficult except for the humble—those who
> believe that they will certainly meet their Lord and
> that they will return to Him.* (2:45-46)

If we claim that we believe in God, that we love Him
and are anxious to please Him, and that we look forward
to meeting Him, our words must be backed by our
actions. It therefore follows that we must think of Him
and turn to Him again and again throughout the day
and night, glorifying Him, thanking Him, and asking for
forgiveness, help, support and all our needs from Him.

> *Those who are patient, seeking the Face of their
> Lord, and are regular in salat, and spend [in charity]
> out of what We provide for them secretly and openly,
> and turn away evil with good — theirs will be the
> reward of the [Eternal] Home.* (13:22)

> *And your God is one God; therefore, surrender to
> Him. And give good news to the humble, those whose
> hearts feel fear when God is mentioned, and those who
> are patient with whatever befalls them, and those who
> are regular in salat and spend [in charity] out of what
> We have provided them.* (22:34-35)

Surely salat restrains [worshipers] from indecency and vileness, and the remembrance of God is the greatest. And God knows whatsoever you do. (29:45)

For those who are want to worship more than the prescribed five times a day, there are other additional times and occasions for *salat*. Especially precious is *salat* in the small hours of the night while others are asleep, the time when we are nearest to our Most Merciful Lord.[44]

CLEANLINESS AND COVERING

God instructs us in the Qur'an to be clean for His worship. There should be no trace of urine, stool or any other filth on our body or clothing. The spot where we pray should also be clean, and we can cover it with a cloth, mat or rug. A brief washing (*wudu*) is carried out before praying (more about this on page 105). Women should be completely covered, excepting their faces and hands.

HOW THE *SALAT* IS OBSERVED

Each of the five prayers consists of a fixed number of cycles or *rakat*s. In each *rakat*, we first stand at attention and recite passages from the Qur'an. Then we bow from the waist, saying silently three or more times, "Glory be to my Lord, the Almighty (*Subhana Rabbi al-Adheem*)." We then prostrate on the floor, saying silently three or more times, "Glory be to my Lord, the Most High (*Subhana Rabbi al-Ala*)." In both the second and the final *rakat*s of each *salat*, we add to this a period of sitting, while glorifying God and invoking blessings upon His beloved Prophet (ﷺ). The *salat* then ends with the Islamic greeting, "Peace be upon you, and God's mercy and blessings (*"As-salamu alaikum wa rahmat-Allahi wa barakatuhu"*).

SUPPLICATION

Muslims also do a great deal of supplication (*du'a*)—that is, informal, personal prayer, during which we speak to our Lord, asking for forgiveness, thanking Him for His favors, praying for others, expressing our concerns, and asking Him for help and for anything we may need, for He says, *"Call Me. I shall respond to you"* (40:60).

There are no limitations on the times and occasions of such prayers. However, it is customary, after concluding the formal *salat*, to sit in our place of prayer, invoking blessings upon the Prophet (ﷺ), glorifying God, and then making our own informal supplication.

Another specially favored occasion for supplication or *du'a* is during prostration in *salat*. Prostration is the most humble posture we can assume in front of our Creator and the one that brings us nearest to Him. "Be earnest in supplication while prostrating yourselves," the Prophet (ﷺ) said, "for it is fitting that your supplications [in that humble posture] should be answered."[45]

Many Muslims carry on a constant internal conversation with God. We can speak to Him in any language, at any suitable time and occasion,[46] with the certainty that He hears and responds.

> *And when My servants ask you [Muhammad]*
> *about Me, I am surely near. I respond to the call of the*
> *supplicator when he calls Me. So let them respond to*
> *Me and let them believe in Me, in order that they may*
> *be rightly-guided.* (2:186)

But sometimes our prayers are not answered or the answer is different from what we hoped for. In such a case, we can be sure that it is not because our Most Merciful Lord has ignored us or rejected our request. Rather, it may be because we've asked for something which He knows is not good for us, or He may have reserved the answer to it for another time and place which is more suitable, possibly in the life-to-come.

SALAT DURING ILLNESS OR TRAVEL

Regular *salat* becomes an obligation for every Muslim, both male and female, by the age of ten. If for any reason one is unable to observe a prayer at the proper time, it is to be made up as soon as possible afterwards. However, women are temporarily exempted from praying during menstruation and the period of bleeding following childbirth; the prayers missed at such times are not to be made up later.

If one is ill or incapacitated, it is permissible to observe *salat* sitting, standing or lying down, and to replace the washing preceding prayer (*wudu*) with a dry cleansing (*tayammum*). Then, if one is traveling, prayers can be shortened and combined—that is, a four-rakat prayer is abbreviated to two *rakat*s and two consecutive prayers are performed immediately one after the other.

Since *salat* is obligatory when its time arrives, Muslims tend to be quite resourceful in finding places for observing their prayers. Hence, even in this country, it's no longer unusual to see Muslims praying in outdoor places or in offices, schools, hospitals, airports or aircraft.

CONGREGATIONAL PRAYER

It is preferable to observe *salat* in congregation rather than alone, whether in a mosque (*masjid*) or at home with the family. For men, attendance at the noon-time congregational mosque prayer on Friday (*Jumah*) is obligatory unless one has a valid reason for being absent (see page 83 for details).

3 THE POOR-DUE (*ZAKAT*)

The Arabic word "*zakat*" means "purification". With respect to this obligatory act of worship, *zakat* refers to the purification of one's wealth by giving a specified share of it to those in need. Since no equivalent to this word exists in English, it is often translated as "the poor-due," "poor tax," or simply as "alms".

The obligation of *zakat* is so important that God mentions it over and over in the Qur'an together with the obligation of *salat*. For while our worship is the right of our Creator, a share in the wealth which He has entrusted to us is the right of the less fortunate.

Since everything we have has been entrusted to us by our Lord, we are not the real owners of anything. Everything is God's, and He has prescribed that a small portion of what He has granted to us be given in charity. Then, when the rightful share of others in our wealth has been paid, all that remains is purified for own use. God says:

> *Truly, the human being was created uneasy, anxious when evil touches him and holding back when good touches him—excepting the worshipers, those who are constant in their salat; and those in whose wealth there is a well-known right for the beggar and the deprived one; and those who testify to the [certainty of] the Day of Judgment; and those who fear the punishment of their Lord.* (70:19-27)

In the Qur'an, God prescribes that *zakat* is to be given to those who are so needy that they do not have the basic necessities of life; to travelers in need; to relieve Muslims of debt; to those serving the cause of Islam; for fighting in a righteous, Islamic cause; and for other works that benefit Muslims. It may either be given directly to needy individuals or through a mosque or other Islamic institution which collects and distributes *zakat* funds.

Zakat is paid on excess wealth but not on articles in everyday use such as one's house, car, furniture, clothing, etc. The categories on which it is to be paid include savings, stocks, gold and silver above the exempted minimum, rental properties, inventory of goods, crops and livestock. It is due on these at a rate of 2-1/2 per cent after they have been in one's possession for a full year.

VOLUNTARY CHARITY

In addition to the obligatory *zakat*, giving voluntary charity is enjoined in numerous verses of the Qur'an, such as the following:

> *You will not attain righteousness until you spend [in charity] of what you love. And whatever you spend, God surely knows it.* (3:92)

> *If you make known your charity, it is well, but if you hide it and give it to the poor [secretly], it is better for you and will atone for some of your bad deeds. And God is informed of whatever you do.* (2:271)

> *Your wealth and your children are only a test, and with God is a tremendous reward. Therefore, being as mindful of God as you are able, and listening and obeying and spending [in charity] is better for your souls. And those who are saved from the greed of their nafs, those are the successful. If you lend God a goodly loan [by giving in charity], He will double it for you and will forgive you. And God is Most Appreciative, Most Forbearing.* (64:15-17)

4 THE FAST OF RAMADAN (*SIYAM* OR *SAWM*)

Fasting during the month of Ramadan is another prescribed act of worship. Although Muslims often fast at times other than Ramadan, fasting throughout this holy month is an obligation on all sane, adult Muslims, unless they have a condition or are in a situation in which exemptions or alternatives to fasting are permitted.

Fasting is an important practice in most religions, often prescribed as a penance for past sins. But the fast of Ramadan is not for this purpose. Rather, it is prescribed for Muslims as a means of learning to be mindful of God through self-discipline and control of the lower self or *nafs*.

On the physical level, we deny ourselves the satisfaction of otherwise permissible needs during a fixed period—the daylight hours—throughout this month. By this means, we learn to take control of our bodily needs and desires at our Lord's command. This has the effect of freeing up our souls and giving them power over our bodies, with their constant demands for food, drink and sex. This simple physical control in turn becomes a basis for learning to control our eyes, ears, tongues and the passions of our lower selves.

Fasting also teaches us flexibility in our habits and acts as a means of cleansing our bodies. In addition, the temporary experience of hunger and thirst teaches us empathy and concern for those who are permanently hungry and in need.

THE ISLAMIC CALENDAR

Since long before the time of the Prophet (ﷺ), the Arabs used a lunar calendar in which each month begins when the new crescent moon becomes visible. Ramadan is the ninth month of the Islamic year. It was during a night in Ramadan that the angel Gabriel (ﷺ) first appeared to Prophet Muhammad (ﷺ) in the mountain-top Hira cave, bringing him the first revelation of the Qur'an and investing him with prophethood.[47] Concerning this sacred month, God says:

> *The month of Ramadan is that in which the Qur'an was sent down, a guidance for mankind and*

clear proofs of the guidance and the criterion [of right and wrong]. Therefore, whoever among you is present during the month, let him fast. And whoever is ill or on a journey, [let him fast] an [equivalent] period of other days. God desires ease for you and does not desire hardship for you, and that you should complete the period [of fasting], and that you should glorify God for having guided you, and in order that you may be thankful. (2:185)

THE PRACTICE OF FASTING

The customary daily pattern of Ramadan among Muslims is the following: As soon as the sun sets, we 'open' our fast with dates, water, milk or any other light food. This fast-breaking is called *iftar* or *futoor*. We then pray the sunset prayer, have dinner and relax for a while. The night prayer is then observed.

The night prayer is followed immediately by an additional *salat* called *taraweeh*, which is observed only during Ramadan. *Taraweeh* prayer is recommended but not obligatory; it can be performed at home or at the mosque. It consists of either eight or twenty *rakat*s (cycles), performed in sets of twos. In many mosques, the recitation of the entire Qur'an is completed in nightly portions during the *taraweeh* prayers in Ramadan.

The Prophet (ﷺ) recommended having a second meal before the break of dawn to keep up our strength for the day. This meal is called *suhoor* or *sehri*, and it is followed by the dawn prayer. We can then go back to sleep or carry on with the normal activities of the day until sunset, which marks the end of the day and its period of fasting.

RAMADAN, GOD'S MONTH

While Muslims are expected be devoted to God and on their best behavior at all times, Ramadan is special. It is our Lord's holy month. During it, we try to gain control over our *nafs* in a number of ways.

The obligatory, formal fasting is simple fasting from satisfying basic bodily needs during the daylight hours: leaving off, during that period, what is normally permitted—all food, drink and marital relations[48] (however, these are permitted freely from sunset to dawn). But on a deeper level, Muslims are supposed to 'fast' from everything that is displeasing to God: the sins of the eyes, ears, tongue and hand, and every sort of falsehood, backbiting and wrong-doing. The keynote of this month is self-discipline and self-restraint.

In addition to this, Ramadan is the time for intensive reading of the Qur'an. In fact, many Muslims complete the reading of the entire Holy Book during this month. It is also a time of being as generous as possible in giving charity and doing other good deeds. During this month, Muslims often get together in the evening to break fast, eat dinner and pray. Inviting fasting Muslims for the evening meal—especially those without families—is considered a good deed.

SOME CONDITIONS

Fasting becomes an obligation on a Muslim young person by the time he or she reaches puberty. However, in many Muslim families children begin fasting at a much younger age; in fact, young children often consider being allowed to fast a privilege and a mark of maturity. By means of this gradual practice, fasting throughout the entire month will be familiar and routine by the time it becomes obligatory.

If we are traveling and fasting is a hardship, or if we are ill, we may postpone fasting until conditions return to normal. Women are not permitted to fast during menstruation or the period of bleeding following childbirth; however, they must make up the missed days later. During pregnancy or nursing, if fasting is a hardship or is dangerous for the mother or the baby, women are excused but must make up the missed fasts later if they are able. If we are unable to fast at all due to some chronic illness, we pay a 'ransom' in charity, which is equivalent to the cost of one average meal per missed day.

At the conclusion of Ramadan, Muslims celebrate one of Islam's two major festivals, *Eid al-Fitr*, the Festival of Completing the Fast. This is discussed on page 84.

5 THE PILGRIMAGE (HAJJ)

Pilgrimage to Mecca once in a lifetime is the fifth of the prescribed acts of worship. God says, *"Pilgrimage to the House [the Kabah] is an obligation on people toward God, for the one who is able to find a way to do it"* (3:97). Accordingly, *hajj* becomes obligatory for Muslims when their health permits, when they have enough means to make the trip and provide for their dependents in their absence, and when there is safety of travel in both directions.

Hajj is the largest international gathering on earth. During recent years, more than two million Muslims from nearly every country of the globe have gathered in Mecca during the *hajj* season (which moves throughout the year together with the other dates of the Islamic calendar). Among the pilgrims, there are no distinctions of rank. All the races of the world are mingled together, worshiping, living, interacting, eating, sleeping side by side. The Muslim who take part in this pilgrimage feels his or her own personal insignificance as one tiny unit in that immense throng of the worshipers of the Lord of Creation. The *hajj* is a tremendous, moving, unforgettable spiritual experience, as anyone who has experienced it will confirm.

Is Mecca the site of the *hajj* because Prophet Muhammad (ﷺ) was born there? No, it has nothing to do with that. Rather, it's because the prophet Abraham

(ﷺ), together with his son, the prophet Ishmael (ﷺ), built there, at his Lord's command, the first house of worship on earth, the Holy Kabah.[49] To Muslims, Mecca, the site of this Sacred House of God, is the spiritual center of this planet. Consequently, as ordered by God,[50] every Muslim, wherever he or she may be on earth, faces the direction of Mecca during *salat*.

Mecca is possibly one of the bleakest, most inhospitable spots on this earth. The city lies inside a bowl-shaped depression ringed around by stark, jagged black lava peaks on which nothing grows. By the design of the All-Wise Lord, there is nothing at all in the place to attract a tourist or casual visitor. When Muslims go to *hajj*, therefore, they do not go for a vacation or for any worldly enjoyment; they go solely for the sake of God, seeking His forgiveness, mercy and pleasure. Visiting the Lord's Sacred House, whose special radiance deeply affects the onlooker, is one of the greatest happinesses a Muslim can experience.

As for the rites of the *hajj*, they are few and simple, and can be learned by reading any standard book on the subject.

V
ISLAMIC FESTIVALS AND OBSERVANCES

1 FRIDAY (*JUMAH*)

In Islam, there is no day of rest, as in Judaism and Christianity. However, Friday is the most honored day of the week, the day of obligatory congregational *salat*[51] throughout the Muslim world.

The Friday prayer is observed in mosques at the time and in the place of the noon prayer. To prepare for it, Muslims shower and put on clean clothes, following the Prophet's *sunnah* (practice).

When the worshipers are gathered, the leader of the prayer (*imam*) gives a sermon about some topic of interest or importance, and glorifies God, invokes His blessings on the Prophet (ﷺ), and asks for His mercy, help and support. The members of the congregation then line up in rows and pray the two *rakat*s or cycles of the Friday prayer.

2 THE TWO FESTIVALS (*EIDS*)

The Arabic word "*eid*" means "festival". Islam has two major festivals, known as *Eid al-Fitr* and *Eid al-*

Adha. On both festivals, the same general observances are followed.

A special *Eid salat* is held in the morning, at which (according to the Prophet's instructions) all Muslims should be present. In centers of Muslim population, attendance at the *Eid* prayers is so large that the prayer is either held outdoors or in a large meeting hall.

Prior to the prayer, a sermon is given by the *imam*. This is followed by the two *rakats* of the *Eid* prayer, which is marked by several repetitions of "God is Most Great"—in Arabic, "*Allahu akbar*." After the prayer, the worshipers greet and congratulate one another for the occasion.

For each of the two *Eids*, a specific charity is prescribed. This will be detailed below.

The *Eids* are happy, warm occasions, celebrated with enthusiasm and joy. For both festivals, Muslims like to have new clothes or at least to wear their best, and money or presents may be given to children. An important part of the *Eid* tradition is visiting and inviting relatives and friends; there may also be outings, picnics and parties. Each country or region in the Muslim world has special foods for each of the two festivals. Nonetheless, with all these festive traditions, the *Eids* still remain primarily religious holidays.

THE FESTIVAL OF COMPLETING
THE FAST (*EID AL-FITR*)

In the Islamic lunar calendar, the first of the two *Eids*, *Eid al-Fitr*, occurs on the first of Shawwal, the month immediately following Ramadan. This festival celebrates the completion of the month of fasting and marks a return to normal, routine schedules and activities. The celebration of this *Eid* lasts for three days.

The charity of *Eid al-Fitr* consists of a fixed amount of money, due on behalf of each member of the family.[52]

This is to be given to any seriously needy Muslim(s) before the time of the *Eid salat*, either in person or through a mosque or other organization devoted to helping the poor.

THE FESTIVAL OF SACRIFICE (*EID AL-ADHA*)

Eid al-Adha is closely related both to events in the life of the Prophet Abraham (ﷺ) and to the *hajj*. Its celebration lasts four days.

On the day before this *Eid*, the ninth of the Islamic month of Dhul-Hijjah, the pilgrims complete the main rite of the *hajj*—assembling on the plain of Arafat near Mecca, where they spend the afternoon praying for forgiveness and mercy for themselves and their dear ones. On the tenth, eleventh and twelfth of Dhul-Hijjah, they continue with the rites of the *hajj*. Among these rites is the slaughter of an animal in commemoration of the prophet Abraham's sacrifice of a sheep in the place of his son Ishmael (ﷺ).

Meanwhile, on the tenth of Dhul-Hijjah, Muslims throughout the world who have not taken part in the *hajj* begin the observance of *Eid al-Adha* with the *Eid salat*. Those who are able to afford it carry out similar sacrifices of animals in their home communities. And the charity of this *Eid* consists of a portion of the meat of the slaughtered animal.

One-third is kept for the use of one's own family—and is often used the same day for a feast. Another third is given to relatives or friends (who may return gifts of meat from their own supply). The remaining one-third is given away to needy people. Because of this charity, in many parts of the Third World where meat is very expensive, *Eid al-Adha* may be the only time in the year when the poor are able to enjoy it.

3 THE NIGHT OF POWER
(*LAILAT AL-QADR*)

This marks the night on which the angel Gabriel (҈) brought the first revelation of the Qur'an to the Holy Prophet (҈) in Hira cave. Its exact date is not known. However, the Prophet (҈) advised Muslims to seek the Night of Power during the odd-numbered nights of the last one-third of Ramadan. It is customarily observed on the night preceding the twenty-seventh day of Ramadan, with night-long *salat* and recitation of the Qur'an.

4 THE ISLAMIC NEW YEAR
(*HIJRAH* DAY)

The Islamic year begins with the date of the emigration (*hijrah*) of the Prophet (҈) from Mecca to Medina. Hence, the new year begins on 1 Muharram, the first month of the Islamic calendar. In many places in the Muslim world it is observed as a holiday.

5 THE BIRTH ANNIVERSARY
OF THE PROPHET (*MOULID AN-NABI*)

The Prophet's birthday falls on the twelfth of Rabi al-Awwal, the third month of the Islamic calendar. Due to Muslims' great love and respect for the blessed Messenger of God (҈), the celebration of his birth with various traditional observances is common and much loved in most of the Muslim world.

VI

ISLAMIC VALUES AND QUALITIES

Is there anything that makes Muslims different from others? Yes, if we're conscious, committed Muslims, there should be. And this difference lies not only in our distinctive beliefs and religious practices. It also consists of our values and principles, and the personal qualities and characteristics which originate from them. We will now take a look at what some of these guiding values and personal qualities are.

MINDFULNESS OF GOD (*TAQWA*)

Taqwa is a word used over and over in the Qur'an to describe the primary characteristic of a believer: to be always conscious and aware of God—that we are always in front of Him, and that He hears and sees everything we say and do.

If we really believe this, it should motivate us to be on our best behavior at all times, following the guidance provided by the Qur'an and the Prophet's *sunnah*. For above all things, we most dread our Lord's displeasure,

87

and earnestly desire to send ahead for our souls what is pleasing to Him.

TRUST IN GOD AND SURRENDER

Being a Muslim does not mean merely believing in God's existence. More than that, it means trusting Him for the best outcome of all affairs, as small children unquestioningly trust in their parents to do the best for them. It means surrendering and letting our Lord work as He wills—as He is going to do in any case. It means accepting Him as the driver of the car of our lives instead of being a backseat driver. It means consciously leaving anxiety and worry over our affairs, secure in the knowledge that they are in the best of Hands, and that those Hands will guide us to a safe, secure, blessed destiny.

PATIENCE, THANKFULNESS
AND CONTENTMENT

Because we recognize that all things happen according to our Lord's divine Will and not our own, we try to be patient with His Will as it manifests itself in the events of our lives. In every difficulty or trial, we depend on His mercy, help and support. We thank Him again and again for what He has given us—our life, health, eyes, ears, two feet to walk on, loved ones, freedom, peace, work, money and possessions, food to eat, a home to live in, and all His other countless favors. And we try to be contented with it, whether it is much or little, and to be pleased with Him in everything.

RESPONSIBILITY

When Islam enters deeply into our consciousness, it automatically has the effect of increasing our sense of accountability to our Creator. This means maintaining a constant awareness that we are responsible for everything we do, as well as for our inner state, which may be the most important and challenging aspect of all.

Once we have the certainty that our words and deeds have serious, possibly lasting consequences for our present life and for the Eternal Life, it should make us more careful, wise, and less likely to act impulsively or carelessly. Moreover, we should be ready to accept responsibility for everything we've been given—our lives, our bodies, families, work, possessions, status, time, energy and everything else—knowing that all of these constitute a trust from God, and that keeping this trust is our obligation.

SINCERITY

What is sincerity? Sincerity basically means to be as we seem, to do as we say and to say as we do, with only one face toward God and our fellow human beings.

Being sincere with God means that we act for His sake alone,[53] not out of the desire for show, prestige, power, fame or any worldly reward or gain. And being sincere with other people means the same: to act from the heart, not with any hidden motive or the desire to gain something or make use of others—the opposite of acting from 'political' motives. And it means giving our best and doing our best because we deeply care about the quality of whatever we present to our beloved Lord.

HONOR, INTEGRITY, DIGNITY
AND SELF-RESPECT

Committed Muslims are likely to be people who value their honor and integrity above all things and who do not associate themselves with anything that they regard as low or dishonorable. This high standard of honor and integrity, which we try to maintain in all our dealings, is in turn the basis of our dignity and self-respect. Prizing these basic qualities of character so highly, we try not to put ourselves in situations which can lower us in the sight of our Lord, other people or our own selves. For we know that, once lost, honor, dignity, integrity and self-respect are difficult to regain, and therefore we zealously do our best to preserve them.

COMPASSION AND MERCY

These are two of our Lord's chief attributes. Consequently, we, as His servants, should do our best to emulate these divine qualities. Moreover, as we hope for God's mercy upon ourselves, we should try to be compassionate to people, to act in a merciful manner toward all creatures, and to always desire and pray for good for others. Our way of regarding our fellow human beings should be broad and universal rather than limited and chauvinistic. Thus, we should feel concern and compassion for all the world's people, not just our own, empathizing with others' needs and pain, and doing whatever we can to help.

HUMBLENESS

Among the most detestable of all characteristics are pride and arrogance. A Muslim is expected to be humble and modest concerning his or her achievements, and not to boast or show off. To feel superior to others is to follow in the footsteps of Satan, who was cast out of Paradise because of pride and envy.

PURITY

The Muslim's self-respect is largely tied up with his or her inner and outward purity. Consequently, it is of the utmost importance to keep a clean heart, free of dirty, uneasy feelings, and to avoid any action, even the smallest, which could lead to impure thoughts and, above all, deeds. Central to this is avoiding situations which lead to prohibited sexual feelings and actions.

CONTROLLING ANGER, TOLERANCE AND FORGIVENESS

There are two kinds of anger: anger for the sake of God and anger for the sake of our *nafs*. As physicians and behavioral scientists know, the anger of our ego is dangerous and destructive; hence, it must be controlled and if possible eradicated, not let out on others.

Nurturing enmity, resentment and hatred are signs of a heart that needs to be purified. As our Lord is so endlessly forgiving and forbearing, we, His servants, are asked to be tolerant, and to overlook and forgive the mistakes of others. Our focus should be on our own faults, not on other peoples'. Therefore, the faults of others, if known to us, should be kept hidden, not pried into and publicized.

CHARITABLENESS, GENEROSITY AND HOSPITALITY

As we have seen, charitableness is very strongly emphasized in Islam. Generosity in giving, open-handedness in taking care of the needs of others, hospitality toward one's guests—these virtues are central to Islam. At the same time, avoiding extravagance, wastefulness and show are equally important. Both miserliness and ungenerous behavior, and giving rein to the endless desires of the *nafs*, are to be kept strongly in check.

GOOD MANNERS

The Messenger of God (ﷺ) was the finest model of good manners and perfection of character. Hence, the closer Muslims can come to following his example, the greater the honor for them. From the detailed record of the Prophet's actions and sayings—that is, the collections of *hadith*—we know the behavior appropriate to various occasions and kinds of people.

Good manners toward our Lord means being humble

in the face of His endless greatness, respectful and obedient to His commands, patient under difficulties and tests, thankful for His countless favors, contented with whatever He grants us, and sharing His bounties with others. Good manners toward people means being gentle, polite, kind, helpful, cooperative and considerate to the point of preferring others over ourselves; being patient, even-tempered and good-humored; appreciating goodness and overlooking faults; and carefully avoiding anything which could harm or annoy others.

RESPECT

Respect for others is also an important Islamic quality. Since God has honored us, the Children of Adam,[54] likewise we must give honor and respect to one another. This respect is not based on people's race, gender, position or economic status, on what they do or do not do, or what rank they are given by society, which judges by externals. Rather, it is their due as creations of our Lord's, into whom He breathed something of His divine Spirit[55] and to whom He gave immortal souls. Therefore, when we respect others, we are actually respecting God, the Creator of all. However, Islam especially stresses respect for our parents, relatives, teachers, those who are more pious, wiser or older, or who possess more knowledge, especially of the religion.

GOOD WILL

To desire and pray for success, happiness and forgiveness for all of God's servants is a mark of faith, in keeping with the well-known *hadith*, "None of you believes until he desires for his brother what he desires for himself." In contrast to this, envy, jealousy and wishing evil for others are detestable characteristics, inspired by Satan, which we must try to eliminate from our hearts.

BROTHERLINESS

The Muslims of the world, representing nearly every ethnic group and language, make up one community or *ummah*, in which every Muslim is a brother or sister to every other Muslim.

While a vast diversity of cultures and languages exists among Muslims, barriers of race or color have no place in Islam. Rather, the variation of languages and colors among the family of mankind is regarded as a sign of God's endless creativity and art.

> *And among His signs is the creation of the heavens and the earth, and the differences in your languages and your colors. Surely in that are signs for people of knowledge.* (30:22; also 35:28)

The brotherhood and lack of racial tension among Muslims is one of the most attractive features of Islam— the thing that, more than anything else, drew Malcolm X to a new and correct understanding of the religion.

LOVE OF LEARNING AND KNOWLEDGE

"My Lord, increase my knowledge," the Prophet (ﷺ) prayed. And he said, "Seeking knowledge is an obligation on every Muslim, male and female, even if it be in China." Hence, Muslims have traditionally prized and striven to acquire knowledge.

Knowledge is of two kinds, religious and secular. The most valuable kind of knowledge, however, is that which helps us earn God's pleasure and contribute to the good of His servants.

VII
MORALS AND BEHAVIOR

*I*t is not righteousness that you turn your faces
toward the East and the West [in salat]; but rather
the righteous [person] is the one who believes in
God and the Last Day and the angels and the
Scripture and the prophets; and gives [his or her]
wealth, out of love of Him, to relatives and orphans
and the needy and the traveler and those who ask and
[for the freeing of] slaves; and is regular in salat and
gives zakat; and the keepers of their promises when
they promise, and the patient under hurt and injury
and time of stress. Those are the ones who are true;
those are the ones who are mindful of God. (2:177)

As we shall see in this section, Islam relates not only
to beliefs, practices and values. In actuality, it is a complete, all-inclusive system of life in which all aspects are
regarded as part of an indivisible whole. Consequently,
a Muslim is expected to judge everything by one criterion—God's. This means not having one set of behaviors
for so-called 'secular' matters and another for what are
generally considered 'religious' matters, because in
Islam, religion includes everything.[56] Nothing is 'non-
religious' because everything is for God. According to

this understanding, everything a Muslim does is considered as worship if it's done with the intention of pleasing God and in keeping with His laws.

1 REGARDING GOD'S LAWS

Obviously no group can function without a system of rules for regulating its people's behavior. Most of us follow the laws of our government (or society, family, workplace or organizations to which we belong), and if we should decide not to, the consequences are well-known. And just as human governments make laws for their citizens, so God, the divine Law-Giver, makes laws and rules for His servants[57]—and for disobeying those, too, there are well-known consequences.

The laws and rules of Islam are not tied to the historical stages of mankind. Rather, they are for all people, of all times and places. For although the details of life and culture change, the nature of good and evil never changes; nor does the nature of the human being, with its various complex and interrelated facets, which are known only to its Creator.

It's important to understand that God doesn't make rules for mankind to put us into hardship—quite the contrary. Who can possibly know what is ultimately good or bad for us? Obviously, only God. If He did not make rules for us, we'd probably end up doing all the wrong things, imagining that they were right. *"Perhaps you may hate a thing, whereas it is good for you, and you may love a thing, whereas it is bad for you,"* (2:216). Therefore, it's important to understand that all the laws and rules our Creator has prescribed are only for our safety, well-being and good in this world and in the Hereafter.

2 THE PERMISSIBLE (*HALAL*) AND THE PROHIBITED (*HARAM*)

Islam's moral code is not at all vague or open-ended; on the contrary, it is very clear and specific. Actions and things are labeled in plain categories: permissible (*halal*), meritorious, neutral, detestable or prohibited (*haram*). These categories are derived firstly, from the Holy Qur'an and, secondly, from the Prophet's *sunnah*: what he himself did, said, recommended, approved or disapproved of in others.[58]

In Islam, whatever is good and useful is *halal*, whereas whatever is harmful or evil is *haram* (and because good things/actions are much more numerous than harmful ones, most things are *halal* rather than *haram*). If anything is prohibited as harmful, some other, beneficial things are permitted in its place, so that whatever is prohibited is not necessary.[59] Anything that leads to *haram* is likewise *haram*, and doubtful things are to be avoided. Good intentions do not make *haram* things *halal*. And whatever is *haram* is forbidden to everyone alike, regardless of rank, wealth or any other criterion.

3 THE ISLAMIC RULES OF CONDUCT

The principal rules governing a Muslim's behavior toward God and other human beings are as follows:

TREATING HUMAN LIFE AS SACRED

Killing, except in self-defense or in a righteous war, is one of the greatest sins and crimes (in the case of capital crimes, life may only be taken only by the state, following a fair trial). Taking one's own life is also a terrible sin.

In war, fighting is to be strictly between military forces. Acts of terrorism or attacks on civilians are strictly prohibited and detestable in Islam, even if they should happen to be done by individuals claiming to be Muslims.

RESPECTING OTHERS' PROPERTY

Islam insists on strict respect for the possessions of others. Stealing or misappropriating others' possessions, whether by fraud, bribery or any other means, is prohibited.

EXERCISING SELF-DISCIPLINE
AND SELF-CONTROL

Muslims are expected to take responsibility for controlling their desires and behavior. Failure to discipline one's desires and appetites, wastefulness and over-indulgence in luxuries are considered detestable.

KEEPING TO PURITY,
MODESTY AND CHASTITY

Women's dignity and honor is very strongly stressed. Marriage is highly encouraged to provide a permissible, honorable outlet for the sexual needs of men and women, and any form of sexual contact outside marriage is prohibited. Fornication, adultery and prostitution are considered grave sins which attack the foundation of a wholesome society. Homosexuality, bisexuality and transvestitism are regarded as major sins and as perversions of the intrinsic male or female nature decreed and given by God to each individual; as He declares, *"He created the two spouses, the male and the female"* (53:45; also 49:13, 75:39; 92:3).

BEING TRUTHFUL, HONEST AND TRUSTWORTHY

Islam insists on total uprightness in all a Muslim's dealings. Truthfulness and keeping promises, commitments and trusts is required. Lying, cheating, failing to keep promises and trusts, and any type of dishonest dealing are prohibited and detestable.

KEEPING TO FAIRNESS AND JUSTICE

Muslims are ordered to stand strictly for fairness and justice, regardless of whether their own selves, family members, friends or even enemies are involved.[60] The same uniform standard of impartial justice is to be applied to everyone without consideration of race, religion, gender, rank, wealth or any other criteria. Dealing unjustly with others for the sake of one's own self-interest, or because of one's personal bias or other people's mediation, is not permissible. Muslims are also supposed to resist and fight against injustice in all its forms.

FORGIVING PERSONAL INJURIES

God permits Muslims to retaliate for an injuries, but only in a strictly just manner. This means that retaliation may be carried in the precise amount of the injury inflicted but no more, and only against the doer himself. Blood-feuding and taking revenge on people or groups connected to the doer of an injury are strictly condemned and prohibited.

However, although retaliation in kind is permissible, forgiveness for injuries is recommended as being the best course, earning the one who forgives God's pleasure and reward.[61]

REFRAINING FROM HARMING OTHERS

God, the Most Merciful, prohibits Muslims from doing anything which harms His servants, whether by their hands or tongues. We have already looked at the major offenses against others, such as killing, stealing and lying. Other prohibited behaviors include acts of violence and cruelty, harshness, rudeness and putting down others. Backbiting, (which the Prophet defined as saying something about others which they would not want said), spying, suspicion and violating others' privacy are prohibited.[62] The Prophet (ﷺ) said, "Part of the excellence of a person's Islam is that he leaves alone whatever does not concern him."[63]

God also prohibits being sarcastic and mocking, slandering or calling others by offensive nicknames.[64] Using foul and abusive language, "gutter talk," cursing, swearing and insulting others are not acceptable behaviors in Islam.

CARRYING ON BENEFICIAL ECONOMIC ENTERPRISES

All economic practices which keep wealth in circulation, such as industry, agriculture, trading in *halal* goods, distribution of goods and services, and investment in *halal* stocks, are permitted and encouraged. In contrast to this, gaining wealth by any *haram* means, such as giving or taking interest (including bonds), bribery, fraud, betting, gambling, the lottery, prostitution, pornography, trading in *haram* goods such as pork, alcohol or intoxicating drugs, and anything else which harms other human beings or the environment, is forbidden. Also prohibited is practicing magic, witchcraft, fortune telling and astrology (believing in the latter two is also prohibited), whether for gain or not.

BEING PRODUCTIVE AND CONTRIBUTING TO THE GOOD OF SOCIETY

"The human being shall have nothing but what he strives for" (53:39) is an often-quoted verse of the Qur'an. Accepting responsibility, working for the good of others, and putting forth one's best effort is the Islamic standard. Muslim men and women are both expected to be useful and productive, although perhaps in different spheres.

No form of work is considered degrading or beneath our dignity as long as it is honest and does not involve anything prohibited. On the other hand, sitting passively and taking handouts when we are capable of doing something useful, no matter how humble it may be, is detested.

ENJOYING FOOD AND DRINK IN MODERATION

These are permissible pleasures, but excesses are to be avoided. The Prophet (ﷺ) said, "No man fills a worse vessel than his stomach; a few mouthfuls are sufficient for a person to keep his back straight. But if he wants to fill his stomach, he should divide his stomach into three parts, filling one-third of the belly with food, another third with drink, and leaving one-third empty for easy breathing."[65]

Any clean, pure food or drink is allowed, and Muslims enjoy good food of all kinds. Prohibited substances include pork and its by-products, such as lard and animal gelatin, and anything which clouds the mind, such as alcohol in any form and intoxicating drugs. The use of tobacco is considered detestable, if not prohibited. And while gluttony and over-indulgence in food or drink is detestable, at the same time wasting food, even in small amounts, is considered a sin.

SPENDING IN A REASONABLE MANNER UPON ONESELF OR ONE'S FAMILY

Fulfilling one's reasonable needs and desires is permissible as long as one avoids extravagance, and honors the right of the poor and needy upon one's wealth. Material things are not to become a Muslim's preoccupation or goal in life. Excessive love of wealth or possessions, miserliness and hoarding are all detestable.

COOPERATING FOR GOOD, ENJOINING WHAT IS RIGHT AND FORBIDDING WHAT IS WRONG

These are Islamic obligations. A Muslim is expected to feel a sense of responsibility for the state of his family, community and society. Giving good advice is encouraged; however, it must be given with wisdom, tact and understanding. All cooperation for evil purposes is prohibited.

Lack of concern for and failure to try to change what is wrong in society is a breach of responsibility. The Prophet (ﷺ) said, "The one among you you who sees something detestable should change it with the help of his hand; and if he does not have strength enough to do that, then he should do it with his tongue; and if he does not have strength enough to do that, then he should detest it with his heart, and that is the least [degree] of faith."[66]

RESPECTING AND CARING ABOUT ALL OF GOD'S CREATION

Since the Creator has placed the whole world under mankind's control, Muslims are expected to value, preserve and utilize the environment in the best way possible. As our Lord's stewards, we must take seriously our responsibility toward other creatures and all of the natural world. Hence, ecological and conservation practices are highly desirable from the Islamic point of view, while wastage of resources and harmful exploitation of nature are detested.

Animals are also our Lord's creatures, with their own God-given role and purpose. Consequently, Muslims are prohibited to kill animals for sport or mistreat them in any way. When an animal is killed for food, it is to be done swiftly and in as merciful a manner as possible.

All of the above show us how far-reaching and inclusive the Islamic rules for living are. Everything is spelled out clearly; nothing is left to guesswork or chance, or to an individual's own personal notion of what is right and wrong. There is no question that a return to these rules—the rules upon which human civilization was built—would halt the frightening moral decline of society and bring mankind back to a stable and productive course.

VIII

CLEANLINESS AND HYGIENE

Islam places great stress on cleanliness. The Prophet
(ﷺ) said, "Cleanliness is half of faith."[67] Accordingly,
our bodies should be kept clean, our clothing should
be clean, and the inner space of our houses should be
free from the dirt of both the outside and the toilet
area.[68]

What follows is a brief summary of the Islamic rules
of hygiene and cleanliness: for worship, for the toilet and
for sexual relations.

1 CLEANLINESS FOR WORSHIP

For acts of worship such as praying, reading the
Qur'an or making *dhikr*,[69] it is important always to be
in a clean (*taher*) state in front of our Lord, who loves
cleanliness and purity. Our clothing and the place where
we pray must be clean. And our bodies must be cleaned
of anything polluting.

Discharges from the body render us unfit for God's
worship without going through a specific, prescribed
form of cleaning. Again, the details of these forms of
cleaning are practiced according to the example or *sunnah* of God's blessed Messenger (ﷺ).

When we get ready to pray, a brief ablution or washing of the exposed parts of the body, known as *wudu*, is prescribed. Once completed, *wudu* remains intact unless it is broken by any of the following bodily discharges: urinating, having a bowel movement, passing gas, vomiting, and the flowing of blood or pus; sleeping fully or losing consciousness also breaks *wudu*. These constitute the minor pollutions. When any of these occurs, we must make *wudu* again before praying, reading the Qur'an or doing *dhikr*.

Major pollutions occur with sexual relations, a wet dream or any other discharge of semen, and with menstruation and the period of bleeding after childbirth. Following any of these, before we can offer *salat*, fast, read the Qur'an or make *dhikr*, a full-body shower, known as *ghusl*, is required in the place of *wudu*.

2 PERSONAL HYGIENE

In Islam, urine and stool are considered as filth and pollutants. Therefore, when we go to the toilet, it is necessary to make sure that these body wastes do not cling to the body or clothing.

Muslims throughout the world clean themselves with water after using the toilet as a matter of course; in fact, they consider it dirty not to.[70] A jug with a spout is all that is needed for this, or one can attach a spray hose to the toilet; when away from home, one can carry a small empty bottle. The left hand is always used for this purpose; toilet paper can be used with it, but it does not take the place of water. The hands must of course be washed well with soap afterwards.

3 SEXUAL HYGIENE AND RELATED MATTERS

Since sexual relations are an act of love between husband and wife, in addition to satisfying the physical need of both, the Prophet (ﷺ) recommended kissing and loving foreplay before intercourse.

The vagina is the God-ordained place for intercourse. Consequently, it is totally prohibited to have intercourse in the anus. Oral intercourse is considered a detestable, perverted act. Vaginal intercourse with a wife who is menstruating or bleeding following childbirth is also prohibited.

As we've mentioned, showering (*ghusl*) is required of both men and women after intercourse. For a woman, *ghusl* (showering) is also obligatory at the end of menstruation or the period of bleeding following childbirth, both before she can resume praying, fasting, reading the Qur'an and *dhikr*, and also before she can resume sexual relations with her husband.

There are differences of opinion concerning the permissibility of using contraceptives.[71] If they are used, it should be by mutual agreement between husband and wife. The methods used should be of a kind which does not cause harm to the woman or kill an existing fetus. Permanent sterilization is permissible only when there is a serious medical cause. Abortion is prohibited except in a case of clear and serious danger to the life of the mother.

IX
THE FAMILY AND SOCIETY

One of the most emphasized areas in Islam is the family, the basic unit of society. Within it, the foundation of personality is laid down among a circle of relatives bound to one another by ties of blood, mutual affection and responsibility. However, Islam does not define family merely in terms of the Western nuclear family consisting of husband, wife and children. Rather, it includes all relationships by blood and marriage; relatives (including in-laws), whether Muslim or non-Muslim, have special rights on us which non-relatives do not have.

1 MARRIAGE

God created humankind of two sexes in order that men and women may choose spouses, live together in intimacy, and establish new family units. Hence, Islam places very strong emphasis on marriage, according to the command of God: *"Marry the single ones among you"* (24:32). The Prophet (ﷺ) also stressed its importance, saying, "Marriage is a *sunnah* of mine. Whoever turns away from my *sunnah* is not of me." He also said, "When a man marries he has fulfilled half of the religion. Then

let him fear God regarding the remaining half."
Accordingly, marriage—the means of preserving chastity, establishing a family, and finding love, support and
companionship—is the norm among Muslims.

In Islam, marriage is the only permissible outlet for
the sexual needs of men and women; outside it, all forms
of sexual or bodily contact are prohibited to both. Sex is
regarded not as an end in itself, but as part of a total
relationship of mutual responsibility—in short, pleasure
is not divorced from commitment. If two people are
interested in each other, they are expected to get married. In that way, they can enjoy an open, acceptable,
halal relationship in the sight of God and society rather
than a *haram* one, which will result in shame and regret
in the Hereafter, as well possibly in this life.

CHOOSING A MARRIAGE PARTNER

In parts of the Muslim world where boys and girls go
to separate schools and have no occasion for meeting,
marriages are arranged by parents, and young people
generally marry without having met beforehand. But
although parents may make the choice on their behalf,
Islam prohibits forcing anyone into a marriage against
his or her will.

While arranged marriages may work elsewhere, they
are clearly not suitable in the West;[72] in fact, sight-
unseen marriages have often proved to be disasters in
this society. Here, Muslim young people are generally
introduced through a mutual acquaintance. Afterwards,
they get to know each other in the company of the girl's
family or other Muslims, since dating or being together
in situations of total privacy is not permitted, according
to the Prophet's saying, "Whenever a man is alone with
a woman, Satan makes the third [among them]," and
"Satan circulates in the body like blood."[73]

Many factors are important in choosing a life-partner: religion; family and upbringing; compatibility of personalities and temperaments; education and interests; physical characteristics such as height, weight and looks; and, for a woman, a man's financial standing. But perhaps most important is a meeting of hearts, feelings of mutual respect, and the life-values of each partner, as these are the ingredients that are essential for a successful marriage.

Before marriage, issues of mutual concern should be discussed between the prospective partners. Any special conditions that either of them wants to mention may be written into the marriage contract. The details which marriage normally involves are then worked out between the couple, generally with the help of their families.

A Muslim woman, whether virgin or previously married, must be given away by a Muslim male guardian who represents her, such as her father, grandfather, uncle or brother. If she does not have such a relative, she can appoint a trustworthy Muslim man in his place for the purpose.

The man is required to give a dower or marriage gift (*mahr*) to the woman according to his means and whatever is mutually agreed-upon between the two of them. It is preferable that this gift be something of value, but if the man's finances are limited, it can be something of little or no monetary value.

SOME IMPORTANT RULES

In the Qur'an, God specifies that a Muslim man may marry either a Muslim, Christian or Jewish woman,[74] but not women of any other faith. Since Muslims accept and honor all the Jewish and Christian prophets, the Jewish or Christian wife of a Muslim would be free to practice her faith without hindrance. However, since

Muslim children are always brought up in their father's faith, marriage to a non-Muslim woman is a step which a man should take only after very serious reflection, since many conflicts can arise over religious issues.

On the other hand, a Muslim woman is permitted to marry only a Muslim. Her marriage to a non-Muslim man is not recognized as lawful in Islam; rather, it is considered as equivalent to adultery.

Why is this so? The reason is that people of other faiths, including Jews and Christians, do not necessarily respect Islam, its practices, its rules or its Prophet (༄). Hence, a Muslim woman married into a Christian or Jewish family might encounter prejudice, disrespect for her faith, or limitations on her ability to practice it. In addition, the faith of her children would be likely to become a major issue. Therefore, if a Muslim woman wants to marry a non-Muslim man, he should first learn about Islam. If he decides to accept it, it should be out of sincerity and with the intention of living by it and raising his future children in it, not simply in order to marry a certain woman. Then, in order for the marriage to be lawful Islamically, he should make the Declaration of Faith (*Shahadah*) before the wedding ceremony takes place.

The marriage of a Muslim, whether a man or woman, must be entered into with the intention of permanence. Temporary, conditional marriage (*muta*) is prohibited by the majority of the schools of Islamic law. A civil marriage license should accompany an Islamic wedding ceremony. The witnesses to the marriage must be Muslims, either two men or one man and two women.

2 THE ROLES OF HUSBAND AND WIFE

God, the All-Knowing Creator, makes it clear in the Qur'an that men and women are equal in front of Him as human souls. Both have the same religious obliga-

tions (apart from the concession given to women's repro-
ductive cycle). Both are equally accountable to Him for
their deeds, and both will be punished or rewarded
equally, according to His saying,

> *Never will I permit the deeds of any doer among
> you to be lost, whether male or female. You are [part] of
> one another.* (3:195)

> *And whoever does righteous deeds, whether a male
> or female, and is a believer—those shall enter Paradise
> and they shall not be dealt with unjustly in the slight-
> est degree.* (4:124; also 16:97; 40:40)

At the same time, God, in His infinite wisdom, has
created men and women with many differences. First,
because we differ in our bodies, each gender excels the
other in certain physical aspects: men do heavy physical
work better than women because their bodies are con-
structed for such labor, whereas women do what no man
can do—bear and nurse children. Significant differences
are also observable in the mental and emotional makeup and functioning of the two sexes.

Therefore, in Islam marriage is seen as a partner-
ship between two human beings with differing but complementary roles and functions. The relationship
between a Muslim husband and wife is based on mutual love, respect, trust, responsibility and harmony, with
each partner fulfilling and supporting the other. God
says,

> *And among His signs is that He created for you
> spouses from among yourselves in order that you may
> find rest in them, and He has put love and mercy
> between you. Truly, in that are signs for people who
> reflect.* (30:21)

And He sets forth a beautiful metaphor concerning the marriage relationship, saying,

They [wives] are a garment for you [husbands] and you are a garment for them. (2:187)

This simile of a "garment" suggests that a husband and wife are to act as a covering, screen and guard for one another from difficulties and from the outside world. Thus, private matters and secrets are to be kept between the two. The marriage relationship is designed to give warmth, pleasure, happiness, peace and support to both.

THE ROLE AND RESPONSIBILITIES OF THE MUSLIM HUSBAND AND FATHER

In the Islamic framework, every group must have a leader, and the family is a social group in its own right. In His perfect knowledge and wisdom, God has assigned the leadership role in the family to man because He created men with certain attributes which make them better suited for it than women. This leadership role is also related to the fact that God has made men responsible for the financial support of their family members—their wives and children, and, if necessary, their parents and any other relatives who may need help.[75]

But even though the man is the head of the family, he should consult with its members and exercise his leadership in a correct and considerate manner. He has rights on his wife and she has rights on him, according to what is fair and just. Husbands and wives are urged to fear God in their interaction. Lack of respect and responsibility, and cruelty or harshness toward one's spouse are very strongly condemned.

Because the woman carries the baby and its nourishment within her body, she is the natural primary care-giver for the child. But at the same time, the husband should be as involved and helpful as possible. It is not a woman's sole responsibility to care for, train and raise children on her own. On the contrary, the father should play a highly supportive, vital role.

Consequently, a Muslim man is expected to recognize the importance and difficulties of motherhood, and not regard them lightly. He should be compassionate, supportive and loving to his wife as she goes through the many trials of pregnancy and childbirth, months of breast-feeding, countless sleepless nights during the children's early months and when they are ill—nursing, nurturing, teaching, training, correcting, advising, being their confidant and their guide to the world. Lending a hand with work and, when necessary, a shoulder to cry on, giving a word of encouragement and love, and showing affection in tangible ways—these can make all the difference between a dry, dull marriage and one in which the spark of love burns clear and bright and strong.

THE WIFE'S RIGHTS AND RESPONSIBILITIES

Islam gives a wife many rights on her husband. Firstly, she has the right to good treatment and consideration from him. Under no circumstances is oppressive treatment, insulting behavior or physical abuse of women or children permissible. The Prophet (ﷺ) said, "The Muslim whose faith is most perfect is the one whose behavior is excellent, and the best among you are those who behave best towards their wives."[76]

Secondly, she has the right to financial support according to her husband's means—if possible, according to what she was accustomed to in her parents' home. She also has the right to not be prevented from bearing his children if she desires them. And she has the right to seek divorce.

The wife is responsible for meeting her husband's sexual needs—and vice-versa. Out of all the women in the world, he has chosen her to satisfy this need, and likewise, she has chosen him as her only sexual partner.

This ensures that neither of the two will look elsewhere for gratification, which in turn safeguards the family and the stability of society.

From her side, the wife is responsible for the management her home, which is her kingdom. This does not imply her doing nothing but housework, for nowhere does the Islamic Law (*Shari'ah*)[77] specify that this is solely the woman's obligation. Rather, it is the duty of the husband to get this taken care of, although customarily women do it out of good will.

The wife is also responsible for managing her husband's finances and property according to his wishes, for not giving away anything of his possessions without his permission, and for not allowing anyone in his house whom he does not wish.

WOMEN'S WORK AND EARNINGS

The Muslim woman is entitled to study and pursue her interests, according to whatever is suitable and convenient. She is also free to work if she wishes or if necessary, as long as her job does not compromise her dignity as a Muslim woman. Decisions regarding these matters should naturally be made in consultation and agreement with her husband. At the same time, it's understood that a woman's primary responsibility—the thing for which she is firstly accountable to God—is toward her family. Even if she has a satisfying and important career, her family comes first.

A Muslim woman's money or property, whether she earns or inherits it, belongs to her without restriction. She is not obliged to use it to support the family, since this is her husband's responsibility (although she may of course help with expenses if she chooses). According to Islamic law, any money she owns is hers to spend, save or give away as she likes, without accountability to anyone except God.

3 PLURAL MARRIAGES

In Islam, keeping to one wife is the standard and preferred form of marriage. However, the All-Wise Creator has given men a very guarded and restricted permission to marry more than one wife, up to a limit of four, if they can keep to the strict conditions of justice and equality required—which is generally extremely difficult.

This permission serves as a means of safeguarding society, the chastity of both men and women, and the well-being of women under various circumstances. For example, following a war, the number of men in a society may be greatly reduced. In such a case, vast numbers of women have no choice except to remain without a husband to give them support and companionship, often having to turn to prostitution to meet their financial and sexual needs. Again, through plural marriage, women who are unmarriageable for any reason can enjoy a legal spouse and a secure home, and bear children who will be supported by their father until adulthood.

Plural marriage may also save the marriage of women who are unable to bear children or who become chronically ill or incapacitated. Without the permission to take another wife, the husbands of such women would be likely to divorce them and take new wives. But due to this realistic and humane provision, a husband can take another wife without giving the first wife the pain of abandoning her and her children. However, plural marriages as a rule give rise to all sorts of problems and tensions for both the man and the women involved. Moreover, since polygamy is prohibited under U.S. law, in this country it is risky and undesirable from a legal standpoint.

A man who is considering marrying more than one woman must always keep in mind the following: that he is responsible in front of God for treating his wives with strict justice, and for keeping them happy and contented; that he is responsible for their financial support; and that he is also financially and morally responsible for any children he may father, no matter how many, until they reach the age of independence. Knowing that one will be held accountable for all this in front of God should discourage anyone from entering into a plural marriage without clear understanding of the issues and the intention of accepting all it involves.

4 DIVORCE

Divorce is permissible for Muslims as a last resort when all efforts to resolve issues and problems fail. The Prophet (ﷺ) said, "Of all permissible acts, the one which is most detestable to God is divorce."[78]

Just as marriage should not be entered into lightly, neither should a marriage be dissolved without extremely serious reflection and carrying out the preliminary measures prescribed by God, especially if there are children. These measures include discussion and attempts at conflict resolution between the husband and wife, and arbitration with representatives from both sides.

If divorce is decided upon, God permits two revocable divorces after which reconciliation can take place, and an irrevocable third divorce as the final step. A divorce should be carried out in strict keeping with the Islamic rules, which can be learned from any reliable Muslim source, and a civil divorce should accompany it.

5 PARENT-CHILD RELATIONS

One of the most important aspects of Islam is the

relationship between parents and children.

Muslim parents are fully responsible for their children—for their physical care, financial support, and training in religion, morals and worldly matters, a huge task. Strong, loving ties between parents and children are the norm, and they continue after children are grown up and on their own.

Obedience, respect and kind treatment of parents are Islamic obligations. Between the two parents, mothers have been given more rights on their children in consideration of the troubles they go through during pregnancy, childbirth, nursing and rearing.[79] With endless compassion for the difficulties of motherhood, the Most Merciful Lord says,

> *And We have enjoined on the human being goodness to his parents. His mother carries him with hardship and gives birth to him with hardship, and the carrying of him and his weaning is thirty months.*[80] (46:15; also 31:14)

The Prophet said, "God's pleasure consists of the pleasure of parents, and God's anger consists of the anger of parents." He also said, "God may postpone the punishment of any sin until the Day of Resurrection excepting disrespect to parents. Its punishment is swift." Indeed, God mentions disobedience, harshness and neglect of one's parents as being among the worst sins, saying,

> *And your Lord has decreed that you worship no one but Him and that you be good to parents. If one or both of them reaches old age by your side, do not say a word of contempt to either of them nor repulse them, but speak to them with kind words. And, out of compassion, lower to them both the wing of humility and say, "My Lord, be merciful to them, as they cared for me in childhood." (17:23-24)*

From all this, it will be realized that breaking the ties of relationship with one's parents, whether they are Muslims or non-Muslims, is an extremely serious sin for a Muslim. If our parents ask us to do something which involves disobedience to God, we must not obey them. At the same time, we must also not abandon them and must continue to treat them respectfully and kindly as far as possible.

> And We have enjoined on the human being good-ness to parents, but if they attempt to make you join with Me [as a partner] anything about which you have no knowledge, do not obey them. You will all return to Me, and I shall inform you about what you used to do. (29:8)

Therefore, when parents become elderly and find it difficult to live alone, it is an obligation on us to support and care for them just as they did for us when we were young. Leaving aging parents to struggle on their own or putting them into nursing homes is not acceptable to our Most Merciful Lord; personal care, compassion and kind-ness up to death are. Now it is *their* turn to be old, but soon it will be ours, and we will need help from our chil-dren just as they do from us.

6 RELATIONS WITH RELATIVES

Maintaining strong family ties with relatives, Muslim or otherwise, is one of the most strongly empha-sized social aspects of Islam. Especially important are close relatives such as grandparents, siblings, and aunts and uncles. If family members are openly hostile to Islam, relations can be kept to a minimum, but only in rare cases can there be an excuse for breaking them off completely.

7 RELATIONS BETWEEN THE SEXES

The society envisioned by Islam is a clean society,

free of all the many varieties of sexual misconduct and anything which may lead to them. Therefore, observing pure, respectful, responsible relations between members of the two sexes is central to the social interaction of Muslims. Since one's spouse is the only person in the world with whom any type of sexual contact is permissible, relations with all other members of the opposite sex are to be free of any sexual undertones.

Free, casual mixing between men and women is not acceptable. Hence, if mixing does take place, physical distances and correct behavior should be maintained. This means that there should be no hand-shaking, hugging, touching or other forms of physical contact. Moreover, sexual innuendo and suggestiveness are also completely unacceptable and out of place in Muslim circles.

ISLAMIC DRESS

Wearing clothing is a human trait; animals do not wear clothes. And humans wear clothing for three primary reasons: for protection from the elements, for beautification, and for modesty, which again is a very human attribute.

Like Judaism and Christianity in former times, Islam is concerned with modesty. As we have seen, this religion emphasizes the dignity and honor of Muslim women, insisting that they be regarded and treated as dignified, respected human beings, not as sex objects.[81] And in order to minimize the attraction between individuals of the opposite sex so that they do not arouse desire in each other, the All-Wise Lord has laid down the basic rules of dress for both Muslim women and men.

The dress Islam prescribes for women is one which covers the head and entire body. It is sometimes compared to the former nuns' habit, or the type of dress shown in pictures or statues of the Virgin Mary. This is known as *hijab*—that is, the Muslim woman's formal or public attire.

Although styles of *hijab* vary from place to place throughout the Muslim world, depending on local traditions and conditions, they all conform to the basic guidelines for covering given in the Qur'anic verses 24:31 and 33:59. Supplementing these is the Prophet's saying that when a woman reaches the age of menstruation, it is not suitable that she should show any part of her body excepting her face and hands.[82] Therefore, the formal dress of the Muslim woman (like the dress in which she prays) should be long, loose and not show the lines of her figure. It should be opaque enough not to show the color of her skin, not so attractive that it draws attention to her, and not be an imitation of the clothing of men or of non-believers.

Since *hijab* is the public dress of the Muslim woman, it's worn whenever she's outside the house, and also indoors if non-Muslim women or men other than her husband and close male blood relatives are present. But her private dress is based entirely on her own taste and wishes. In the seclusion of her home and among other Muslim women, she can dress informally, style her hair, wear makeup, jewelry and so forth to her heart's content. The only condition which needs to be observed in the presence of other women is covering from the navel to the knee. However, exceptions are made for medical necessities.

It's often asked why Muslim men don't seem to have any distinctive form of dress. But indeed, they do, in as many different styles as women's, although there are no Qur'anic directives concerning this.

Males past the age of puberty are required to cover at minimum from navel to knee except in front of their wives, and their clothing should not permit the private parts, front or back, to be visualized. Wearing tight pants, shirt open down the chest, earrings, necklaces, chains and the like is not acceptable. Men should not imitate the clothing of women or of non-believers, and gold and silk are reserved for female use. Wearing a turban or other headcovering is a well-known *sunnah*. The Prophet (ﷺ) also recommended that Muslim men clip their mustaches, while allowing their beards to grow.

To sum up this discussion, when we consider human sexuality, reproduction and family structure, we can only marvel at the amazing creativity, wisdom and generosity of our Creator, who has made sexual enjoyment one of the finest pleasures imaginable. But, today more than ever, it's important for us to understand that this pleasure is not an unconditional right. Correctly understood, it is an incentive and a privilege intended for those who accept the responsibility of a binding, committed relationship.

If the Islamic guidelines were followed, one woman would would be for one man: his desire would be for her alone and hers for him; her beauty would be only for his enjoyment, not for public consumption. The private parts would not be aroused nor the eyes distracted by seeing everywhere what God intended to be covered from sight except in the privacy of the home and bedroom. Children would be born to and grow up with the love, care and guidance of two married, mutually commited parents. Males would grow up accepting full responsibility for their wives and children, and females would value and at the same time be valued for their primary role as care-givers for their young. And a common, God-centered understanding would govern the interaction of husband, wife and children.

This has been, in brief, a summary of the basic rules of Islam— the rules of the All-Knowing Creator for the good of His servants. They are rules which are capable of producing responsible, disciplined individuals and, in turn, societies made up of such individuals. More than this, they are the rules which are the basis of civilized values and behavior worldwide.

X

THE PATH OF EXCELLENCE AND PURIFICATION OF THE SELF

So far, we have been talking about the basic beliefs, worships and rules that are common to all practicing Muslims. However, for some—those Muslims who desire higher levels of excellence—this is just the beginning. For them, striving to come nearer to God is the most important business of their lives.

Perhaps you may know someone of this sort. If so, you may realize how vital this path is to him or her. Such deep believers are described in many verses of the Qur'an, such as the following:

> *Men whom neither trade nor sale diverts from the remembrance of God and being regular in salat and giving zakat. They fear a Day when the hearts and the vision will be overturned—that God may reward them according to the best of what they did, and add even more for them out of His bounty. And God provides for whomever He wills without count.* (24:37-38)

Those who fear their Lord in secret and are in dread of the Hour [of Judgment]. (21:49)

Those whose hearts tremble when God is mentioned, and when His revelations are recited to them, it increases them in faith, and who put their trust in their Lord. (8:2)

The humble, those whose hearts tremble when God is mentioned, and those who are patient despite whatever befalls them, and the constant in observing salat and who spend [in charity] out of what We have provided for them. (22:35)

Indeed, those who are in awe due to fear of their Lord, and those who believe in their Lord's revelations, and those who do not set up anyone as partners to their Lord, and those who give whatever they give [in charity] while their hearts tremble because they are going to return to their Lord—those hasten in doing good and they shall be foremost in it. (23:57-61)

1 THE WAY OF EXCELLENCE (*IHSAN*)

The people described in the verses above are those whose hearts are alive with the love of God and lighted with His light; sometimes it can be seen on their faces. They remain deeply mindful of their Lord in all they do, knowing that He is constantly present with them. They are diligent in glorifying and thanking Him, in asking for forgiveness for themselves and others, and in His remembrance (*dhikr*). And they possess absolute certainty concerning Him and the life-to-come.

This state is known as *ihsan*, the way of excellence. What this excellence consists of is made clear in the following *hadith*:

It is reported that once a stranger came to the Prophet (☙) while he was sitting with some Muslims.

The stranger began to question him about faith (*iman*) and then about Islam. When the Prophet (ﷺ) replied to his questions, the stranger affirmed that he had told the truth. He then asked the Prophet (ﷺ) about excellence, *ihsan*. "It is to worship God as if you see Him, for although you cannot see Him, He surely sees you," the Prophet (ﷺ) replied. After this, the stranger asked the Prophet (ﷺ) about the Hour of Judgment, listened to his answer and departed. The Prophet (ﷺ) asked his companions to call the man back, but they were unable to find him. The Prophet (ﷺ) then said to them, "That was [the angel] Gabriel. He came to you to teach you your religion."[83]

This, then, is the religion of Islam in its highest manifestation: *"To worship God as if you see Him, for although you cannot see Him, He surely sees you."*

Now, suppose we try briefly to imagine ourselves in such a state so that we may better understand the kind of people described in the preceding verses, who are known in Islam as "people of determination."

2 TRYING IT OUT

If we were to be like this, we would believe with total certainty that our Lord is with us at every moment, knowing, seeing and hearing everything we do—and we would always want to present our best to Him, not just any old thing we might happen to have available at the time. The ordinary obligations of the religion would not satisfy us, for we would be asking for a state of extraordinary nearness to God. For example, although we would try to keep a balance in our lives, sleep would not be as important to us as it is to most people because we would want to spend some part of the night alone with our beloved Lord.

Since we would be asking for high ranks, we would try to come closer to our Maker by emulating His blessed

Prophet's countless acts of worship, charity and other kinds of goodness, and to do them in the best way possible. Because we would feel very shy about ourselves, we would regard any so-called 'good' thing that we might do as being totally unworthy of our Lord's greatness and glory. Consequently, we would do such acts in secret and would feel deeply embarrassed if we were ever 'caught' at them.

At the same time, we would feel extremely ashamed of doing—and feeling or thinking—anything that might not be pleasing to our beloved Lord; whatever He does not like in us, we also would not like in ourselves. We would long to come to Him with a clear, clean heart, one in which there would be no trace of anything that is unacceptable to Him. We would try to purify our intentions and to rid ourselves of destructive, harmful feelings such as anger, hate, resentment, bitterness, envy, lust, pride and greed, working to make our spiritual hearts like a clean, clear mirror in which our Lord alone is reflected.

3 FIGHTING AGAINST THE *NAFS*

The Arabic word *"jihad"* means "striving".[84] It is reported that once the Prophet (ﷺ) remarked, when he returned from a battle, "We are returning from the lesser *jihad* [on the battlefield] to the greater *jihad* [within the self]." Consequently, when we are serious about our religion, we are involved in a life-long struggle between our soul and its enemies: Satan, our *nafs*, its passions, and worldly attractions. Part of this struggle involves fighting against negativity and destructive energies, which are tools of Satan, both within ourselves and in our surroundings.

Because we know that disciplining our ever greedy, never satisfied *nafs* is the key to spiritual advancement, we refuse to give in to its perpetual and unlimited desires, and firmly impose the limits of our will upon it. This does not mean denying ourselves necessities or legitimate desires, but rather, becoming the master of our *nafs* instead of its slave.

Voluntary fasting is one of our most useful tools in this effort, for it obliges our endlessly demanding *nafs* to accept the limits we set for it. So is doing good to others, giving of what we love, and cutting out of our lives every harmful and useless activity. We also make war against our *nafs'* unbounded laziness, love of complaining, and ingratitude for God's countless favors.

Our Lord's attributes of love and mercy are the ones we emphasize most. Since He is so endlessly forbearing and tolerant toward us, His often faithless servants, we look at our fellow human beings with the eyes of compassion and understanding, respecting each soul as carrying something of our Lord's divine Spirit. Thus, we try to see the good in everyone, and instead of seeking out others' faults and regarding them as hopeless sinners, we view our own *nafs* as being worse than anyone else's. We base our interaction with our Lord's fellow-servants on love, mercy and tolerance, and desire to do good and be of service to others.

4 SEEKING HELP AND SUPPORT

When troubles and calamities come upon us, we feel the hurt just like everyone else. Nevertheless, we try not to complain. Instead, we choose the path of being thankful for all the good God has granted us and patient with difficulties, for we realize that, as there is ease, there must also be hardship; as there is pleasure, there must also be pain. We remain keenly alert to grasp the lessons and divine wisdoms in all that happens, certain that whatever God sends us is for the best. Knowing that we have no refuge from God except *in* God, we seek help and and comfort in the words of the Qur'an, *salat*, supplication and *dhikr*—the remembrance of God, about which He says,

> *O you who believe, remember God with much remembrance, and glorify Him early and late* (33:41-42),

and,

> *Those who believe and whose hearts find satisfaction in the remembrance of God. Truly, hearts do find satisfaction in the remembrance of God* (13:28).

After this brief journey into the inner world of such Muslims, perhaps we may be able to understand them more easily. People of this sort have sold the life of this world in exchange for their Lord's pleasure and love, and feel happy with the bargain they have made. These are the people who make a real difference in society by inspiring and carrying others, being faithful to their commitments and responsibilities, keeping their honor in every situation, and trying to do whatever they do with excellence. These are also the people who give everything, even life itself when the situation requires it, to keep their commitment to their beloved Lord.

We ask God to make us like such honored and valued people—those to whom, when they meet Him, He will say,

> *O you satisfied soul, return to your Lord, well-pleased, well-pleasing. Then enter among My [faithful and beloved] servants, and enter My Paradise!* (89:27-30).

XI
SUMMING IT UP

These are the teachings of Islam, the basic beliefs and practices of the world's 1.3 billion Muslims. Today, perhaps six million Muslims live in North America. A large percentage of these Muslims are Americans—black, white and every other variety. Islam is currently the fastest growing faith in this continent and in Europe. In fact, there are already more Muslims in the United States than Presbyterians and Episcopalians.

However, I'm not trying to claim that all or even most Muslims are like the ones I described in the last chapter because that's simply not the case. Just as in every other religious community, there are all kinds, from the best to the worst. What I've been telling you about is the religion itself, the way it was revealed by God.

As is evident in everything around us, today two distinct factions are struggling for the domination of our world. One group consists of those who are firmly allied with God. The other, knowingly or unknowingly, consists of the allies of Satan, the source of evil,[85] whom God repeatedly warns us against.[86] And Satan is calling, constantly, insistently calling us to his side.

Some people are answering his call willingly and eagerly, accepting him as their guide. However, others often don't recognize his call for what it is. Perhaps now more than ever before, many people don't understand who is calling them and what he's calling them to. Therefore, it's absolutely critical to understand how Satan works.

He operates hand-in-hand with our *nafs*, inciting us to enmity, anger, hatred, violence, greed, lust and the thirst for power. He lures us on through everything that is dirty, low and dishonorable. And, as he did with our grandparents, Adam (ﷺ) and Eve, he urges us to disbelief and disobedience to our Lord.

He does all this through trickery and deceit, masking falsehood so that it looks like truth and truth so it looks like falsehood. Because Satan is the greatest con artist ever, he knows how to sugar-coat evil and make it so attractive that it's easy to mistake it for good.[87] Once we know this, though, we should be able to realize that unbelief, doubt and anything that is evil, wrong, indecent, harmful or against God's rules is inspired by him.

At the same time, God, our Creator is calling to us, inviting us to believe in Him, accept Him, follow His guidance, and be with Him forever. *"Let them answer My call and let them believe in Me so that they may be rightly guided"* (2:186), He says. *"And God calls to the Home of Peace, and He guides whom He wills to a straight path"* (10:25). And we must make a choice.

The choice before us is either to honor and support the light which He put within us, our immortal soul, or to stamp on it, violate it and try to crush it. It's a choice between the Lord who created us and loves us, and our arch-enemy since the time of our forefather Adam (ﷺ),

who is out to destroy us; between the forces of good and evil; between Paradise and Hell. And we cannot be neutral; we can't take a position in between the two because "in between" is no position. There *is* no middle ground. We're either going to be workers for one side or the other, and we get to decide which we prefer.

"But I'm just one person," you may be thinking. "What I do doesn't matter. It can't affect anything or anyone."

Not so; this is a mistaken notion. Each of us is an integral part of human society, and therefore, whatever we do ultimately has an effect on everyone else. The direction we're going in, what we're committed to, how we conduct our lives—this is our individual contribution to the total pool, the combined energy flow of mankind. There is no escaping our part in it.

If we're going the wrong way, the way of negativity, darkness, defeat and despair, we *can* change, we *can* turn our lives around. The answer to today's problems is not more police, more jails, more rehab programs, better methods of protection against diseases. The answer is more commitment and responsibility.

Every change begins inside our hearts. It starts with an intention, which gets translated into action. It's useless to sit around waiting for somebody else to do something. Each of us has to do it, starting from within.

It's up to us to decide whether we're going to use our time, energy, minds, health, youth, talents and whatever else we've been given for good or evil. Each of us has been granted the privilege and, yes, the awesome responsibility of making such a choice. We're either going to be part of the problem or part of the solution.

Surrender to God's Will and His laws—that is, Islam—*is* that solution. What does it take? Only two things.

The first is to believe that nothing is entitled to our worship, obedience and total devotion except God, our Creator, and that Muhammad, the best of His creation, is His last messenger. And the second is the intention to live by that belief.

This doesn't mean that as soon as someone accepts Islam he or she has to start applying all its teachings— no. That happens over time, according to one's readiness and desire. What it does mean is taking God as our Lord, Muhammad (ﷺ) as our guide and life-example, and the Qur'an as the revelation we live by.

It's not important whether or not there's bad stuff in our past, because our Most Merciful Lord loves to forgive. The Prophet (ﷺ) often spoke about this. He even said that if people did not commit sins, God would remove them and replace them with others who would sin and ask His forgiveness, and He would forgive them.[88] He also said that God's mercy has one hundred parts. Through only one single part of it, there is love among the inhabitants of the earth. The other ninety-nine parts all are reserved for the Day of Resurrection.[89] Reserved for whom? *For us.*

In any case, when we accept Islam by making the Declaration of Faith, we become as pure as a new-born baby in God's sight. At that time, chosen and honored by Him to be among the community living by His final guidance, all our past sins are wiped away and we make a new fresh start with a clean, blank life-book to write on. As the Prophet (ﷺ) once said to a man who wanted to make *Shahadah* but was worried about his past sins, "Do you not know that [accepting] Islam wipes away all the [previous] misdeeds."[90] Now, can anyone possibly imagine anything better than that?

As perhaps you've now realized, Islam is about the highest goodness. Our goal in accepting and living by it is to build a strong relationship of surrender, trust and love for God, our Creator, whom we are going to be with for all eternity. And all our practice of it—every good thing we do, every bad thing we avoid—is only to send ahead for our souls something pleasing to our beloved Lord.

> *There is no compulsion in religion. The right way has been made clearly distinct from error. Therefore, the one who rejects false deities and believes in God has grasped a firm bond which never breaks. (2:256)*

NOTES

¹ See the Holy Qur'an, 32:9 (chapter 32:verse 9), 15:28-29 and 38:71-72.

² This symbol, which means "Peace be upon him," represents the Muslim's traditional invocation of blessings upon prophets and angels.

³ See the Qur'an, 3:6. In this and many other verses, the word *"muslim"* with a small *"m"* refers to those who were surrendered to God and obeyed His revealed guidance in earlier ages, while "Muslim" with a capital "M" refers to the followers of the faith of Islam brought by Prophet Muhammad (ﷺ).

⁴ The Arabic word for "god" is *ilah*. Allah (*al-ilah, the* God) is the proper Name of the One God in Arabic. While in English we can speak of "gods" or even "Gods," there is no plural form of "Allah" because He is the One, Unique, Incomparable Being who has no partners.

⁵ That is, offspring are produced out of the union of two, a male and a female, while God, the Most High, is the unique, partnerless, genderless One, the Creator of all.

⁶ While the word *"nafs"* actually means "self" or "soul," this aspect of the self is referred to in 12:53 as "the evil-inciting [lower] self."

⁷ God speaks of this in the Holy Qur'an, saying, *"We surely offered the trust [of free will and responsibility] to the heavens and the earth, whereupon they declined to bear it and were fearful of it, but the human being bore it. He was indeed unjust and foolish"* (33:72).

⁸ See 2:30, in which God announces to the angels His creation of Adam (﷽), the first man, who represents all mankind, with the words, *"I am surely going to place a vicegerent on the earth."*

⁹ God gives us a clear statement of the purpose of our creation, saying, *"I created jinn and mankind only in order that they might worship [and serve] Me"* (51:56).

10 *"Have you seen the one who takes his desires as his god?"* (25:43), God asks. This should make clear to us what constitutes accepting something as a god in His sight.

11 See 33:43; 42:5.

12 See 43:80; 82:10-12.

13 See 17:14; 23:62; 36:12; 45:29.

14 See 15:27; 55:15.

15 See 72:1-2.

16 See 18:50.

17 The angel Gabriel (﷿) is mentioned by name in 2:97-98 and 66:4. He is referred to as *"the Spirit"* in 70:4, 78:38, 97:4; as *"the Holy Spirit"* in 2:87, 2:253, 5:110/5:113 in some translations, 16:102; and as *"the True* or *Trustworthy Spirit"* in 26:193.

18 On at least one occasion, several of the Prophet's Companions saw the angel Gabriel (﷿) in human form and heard him conversing with the Prophet (ﷺ). This incident is mentioned on pages 126-127.

19 The Qur'an is arranged into verses (*ayah*s), which are contained in chapters (*surah*s) that take their name from something related to or mentioned within the *surah*.

20 It should be noted that native Arabic speakers form only about 18 per cent of the world's 1.3 billion Muslim population.

21 See 2:132-133; 3:19; 3:84-85.

22 Although Adam (﷿) was one single individual, the Arabic word *"aadam"* also means "human being".

23 Remnants of the ark are said to have been found on mountains in eastern Turkey and western Iraq.

24 Muslims' respect for Abraham (﷿) is so great that he is mentioned in a supplication at the conclusion of every prayer (*salat*), following the practice (*sunnah*) of Prophet Muhammad (ﷺ)

25 See 3:45-47; 19:16-21; 66:12.

26 3:46, 48-49; 5:112-115/5:115-118 in some versions.

27 That is, Jews and Christians.

28 Prophet Muhammad (ﷺ) said, "If anyone bears witness that there is no deity except God—He is One and has no partner—and that Muhammad is His slave and His messenger, and that Jesus is God's slave and His messenger and His Word which He bestowed upon Mary and a soul created by Him, and that Paradise is real and Hell is real, God will admit him into Paradise regardless of what deeds he has done." (*Sahih al-Bukhari*, Vol. 4:*hadith* No. 644)

29 The claim that Jesus (﷼) is God, or the Son of God, raises many unanswerable questions. For example, if Jesus (﷼) is God and Jesus (﷼) died on the cross, then it was actually God who died. But how can a being who dies be considered God? And was the universe without a God during that period of His 'death'? And if Jesus (﷼) is God, or even the Son of God, why did he call out to God upon the cross, "My God, my God, why have you forsaken me?" (Matt. 27:46; Mark 15:34).

30 A variation on the name Muhammad (ﷺ), whose root letters, like those of Ahmad, are *h-m-d*, meaning "the praised one."

31 In Islam there is no notion of the inferiority of females due to Eve's having tempted Adam (﷼). Rather, Adam and Eve (﷼) were both guilty of sin, and Satan was equally the tempter of both.

32 The Arabic word *"qur'an"* means "that which is to be read or recited." Thus, the very first word of the first revelation, *"Iqra"* (96:1), meaning "read" or "recite," is intimately connected the name of the Holy Book itself.

33 See 10:37; 13:1; 69:43, 51; 32:2; 33:21.

34 The Prophet (ﷺ) said, through divine inspiration, "When God created the creation, He wrote in His Book [of Decrees]—and He wrote that concerning Himself and it [what He wrote] is placed with Him on His Throne —'Truly, My mercy overcomes My anger.'" (*Bukhari*, 9:501; also 9:642, 9:643)

35 The Prophet (ﷺ) said, "A prostitute was forgiven by God because, in passing by a panting dog near a well and seeing that the dog was about to die of thirst, she took off her shoe, and tying it with her head-cover, she drew out some water for it. Then God forgave her because of that." (*Bukhari*, 4:538)

36 *Bukhari*, 1:39, 1:40, 8:498.

37 *Bukhari*, 9:532(a), 9:532(b).

38 See 17:65; 38:82-83.

39 See 8:28; 64:15.

40 The blessed Prophet (ﷺ) promised, on God's behalf through divine inspiration, expiation of sins for every sorrow or difficulty a believer passes through, even for such a minor thing as being pricked by a thorn (*Bukhari*, 7:544, 7:545; *Muslim*, 6237, 6239, 6243; *al-Muwatta*, 50.3.6). He also said that the believer, whether man or woman, continues to afflicted in person, property and children so that he or she may finally meet God free from sin (*Mishkat al-Masabih*, 1567). Again, he said that when God afflicts a believing servant of His and he praises his Lord for the affliction He has brought upon him, he will rise from his bed as sinless as on the day his mother gave birth to him (*Mishkat al-Masabih*, 1579).

41 The Prophet (ﷺ) said, "God afflicts the one for whom He desires good (*Bukhari*, 7:548; *al-Muwatta*, 50.3.7). Again, he said, "When God has previously decreed a rank for His servant which He has not attained by his action, He afflicts him in his body or his property or his children" (*Abu Dawud*, 3084). And he also said, speaking on behalf of God through divine inspiration, "Son of Adam, if you show endurance and seek your reward from Me in the first affliction, I shall be pleased with no less a reward than Paradise for you" (*Mishkat al-Masabih*, 1758).

42 In Arabic, these words are "*Inna lil-Lahi wa inna ilayhi rajioon*" (2:156). They are said by Muslims upon hearing the news of a death or calamity. The Prophet (ﷺ) said, "If any Muslim who suffers some calamity says that which God has commanded, [namely,] "'Surely we belong to God and to Him we shall return.' O God, reward me for my affliction and give me something better in exchange for it,' God will give him something better than it in exchange." (*Muslim*, 1999)

43 While this is not so common in the West, in much of the Eastern world it is part of the normal daily pattern.

44 The Prophet (ﷺ) said, "Each night, when the last one-third of the night remains, our Lord, the Blessed and Most High, comes to the heaven nearest to this world, saying, 'Who is calling on Me, so that I may respond to his call? Who is asking of Me, so that I may give to him? Who is asking for My forgiveness, so that I may forgive him?'" (*Bukhari*, 2.246)

45*Muslim*, 970.

46 The exceptions are when one is in the bathroom or engaged in sexual activity.

47 This night is known as the Night of Power (*Lailat al-Qadr*).

48 This should be understood to mean marital relations, since sexual relations outside of marriage are in any case totally prohibited. The use of tobacco in any form, ordinarily considered to be a detestable habit, is also prohibited during fasting.

49 The word "Kabah," which describes the structure, means "cube" in Arabic. According to Islamic tradition, in the time of Adam (ﷺ), God sent a sacred stone from Paradise at the site of the present Kabah. Using that stone, Adam (ﷺ), the first prophet, built the original House of God, which later disappeared from view. Thousands of years later, God revealed the sacred site to the prophet Abraham (ﷺ), who rebuilt the House of God on it, incorporating the heavenly stone into its structure.

50 See 2:144, 149-150.

51 Attending Friday prayer at the mosque is an obligation for males but optional for females.

52 In former times, the charity of *Eid al-Fitr* was given as a specific measure of grain. Today, in the Western world, the cash equivalent of a standard meal, paid on behalf of each member of one's family, is substituted for this.

53 See 76:5-9; 92:17-20.

54 See 17:70.

55 See 15:29; 32:9; 38:72.

56 Thus, for example, it is not acceptable to wear one kind of clothing for going to the mosque but something completely opposite to that for going to the beach. Likewise, it is not correct to watch or listen to something on television or the stage which it's prohibited to look at or listen to in ordinary life. If it's wrong for us to do it, it's also wrong to passively participate by watching or listening to it.

57 In fact, the laws and norms of civilized society are based upon and closely follow the laws of God.

58 All this is recorded in the books of *hadith* or sayings of the Prophet (ﷺ), which cover a tremendous variety and range of subjects.

59 For example, while pork and alcohol are prohibited due to their harmfulness, Muslims are free to choose from a variety of other, harmless and beneficial meats and drinks.

60 See 4:135.

61 See 5:45/5:48 in some translations; 7:199; 15:85; 42:37, 43.

62 See 49:12.

63 *Al-Muwatta*, 47.1.3; *Mishkat al-Masabih*, 4839.

64 See 49:11.

65 *Mishkat al-Masabih*, 516[R] and 5192.

66 *Muslim*, 1:79.

67 *Muslim*, 1:432, *Mishkat al-Masabih*, 296.

68 For this reason, in many places in the Muslim world, people take off their shoes at the door of the house and wear slippers or go barefoot indoors, using washable sandals in the bathroom.

69 *Dhikr* (*zikr*) or *dhikr-Allah* refers to the remembrance of God by repeating phrases of glorification or His holy Names.

70 In Muslim countries, a water faucet for cleaning is always found within reach of the toilet.

71 In the Prophet's time, the practice of withdrawal was used by some Muslims, and he neither approved of it nor forbade it.

72 Even though it is the custom in many Muslim societies, Islam does not prescribe this way of initiating a marriage. This is made clear by the fact that the Prophet (ﷺ) once asked a Muslim who had proposed for a woman if he had looked at her. When the man replied that he had not, the Prophet (ﷺ) said, "Then look at her, for it is better that there should be love between you." (*Mishkat al-Masabih*, 3107; *Abu Dawud*, 2077)

73 *Mishkat al-Masabih*, 3118; *Muslim*, 5404.

74 See 5:5/5:6 in some translations. "People of the Book" refers to Jews and Christians, those who were sent divinely-revealed scriptures through their prophets prior to Islam. Because of the common belief in God, Muslims have a special relationship with them which includes the permission to marry their women.

75 Muslim men are generally pleased and proud of being able to provide for their families. This is not only a commonly-accepted practice but a religious obligation and a matter of a man's honor and self-respect as well.

76 *Mishkat al-Masabih*, 0278(R), 0628(R), 3264. The Prophet, who was both Almighty God's representative on earth and the ruler of the Muslims, was the ideal example of a husband. In spite of the enormous load of responsibilities he bore, he nevertheless found time to amuse his young wife Aisha. His wives discussed matters and even argued with him at times. In his spare time, he used to help them with the housework, and he milked the goats and mended his own clothes.

77 The Sacred Law of Islam, which is derived from the Qur'an and the *sunnah* of the Prophet (ﷺ), with the consensus of early Islamic scholars and analogy to similar situations serving as supplementary sources.

78 *Abu Dawud*, 2173, 2172; *Mishkat al-Masabih*, 3294.

79 This is made clear from *hadith*s in which a man asked the Prophet (ﷺ) who was most deserving of good from him. The Prophet (ﷺ) replied, "Your mother." The man repeated the question three times and each time received the same answer. When the man asked the question the fourth time, the Prophet (ﷺ) replied, "Your father, and then your other relatives in order of relationship." (*Bukhari*, 8:2; *Abu Dawud*, 5120)

⁸⁰ That is, the months of pregnancy, nursing and the child's total dependence upon its mother. Muslim babies are ordinarily breast-fed, and it is up to the parents to decide on the time of weaning. However, two years is the maximum period of nursing permitted in Islam.

⁸¹ Hence, exploiting female sexuality for advertising and other commercial purposes is extremely objectionable from an Islamic standpoint.

⁸² *Abu Dawud*, 4092. Covering the face and hands for greater privacy is an option but it is not an Islamic requirement.

⁸³ *Muslim*, 1:1; *Bukhari*, 1:47, 6:300.

⁸⁴ The common English rendering of *"jihad"* as "holy war" is mistranslation. The word *"jihad"* actually means struggle, striving, endeavor or exertion. It may refer to exertion either by force of arms, writing, speaking, or the ongoing spiritual struggle within oneself.

⁸⁵ According to Islamic tradition, before he rebelled against God and became the leader of the forces of evil, Satan (or Iblis) was among the angels in Paradise. However, he was not an angel but a *jinn* (see page 26). Full of pride because of his knowledge and worship, he rebelled against God's order to show respect to Adam (﷼) and thus was cast out of Paradise. The story of Satan's rebellion against God is found in 2:30-39, 4:117-121, 7:11-27, 15:26-42, 17:61-65, 18:50, 20:115-116, 38:71-84.

⁸⁶ The warning against following Satan because he is mankind's open enemy is repeated in three verses of the Quran: 2:168, 2:208 and 6:142. Other warnings are found in 4:38, 76; 7:22, 27; 12:5; 17:53; 35:6; 36:60; 43:62.

⁸⁷ God speaks about this in many Quranic verses, such as the following: *"Then do not let the life of this world deceive you, nor let the Deceiver deceive you about God"* (31:33, 35:5); *"Satan desires to lead them far astray"* (4:60); *"Whoever takes Satan as his friend has incurred a clear loss. He makes*

promises to them and stirs up [evil] desires in them, and Satan makes promises to them only as deception" (4:119-120, 17:64); and *"Satan made their deeds attractive to them"* (16:63, 6:43, 27:24). See also 2:268, 8:48, 24:2, 43:36, 58:10.

[88] *Muslim*, 6620-6622; *Mishkat al-Masabih*, 0442(R), 1324, 2332, 2339.

[89] *Muslim*, 6629-6632.

[90] *Muslim*, 220.

GLOSSARY OF TERMS

Adhan (*azan, ezan*): the call to prayer (*salat*).

Allah: the proper Name of God in Arabic.

Allahu akbar (*takbeer*): the phrase, "God is Most Great," which begins every prayer (*salat*) and is repeated with each change of posture throughout it. Muslims also use it informally to express God's greatness.

Ashhadu an la ilaha illa-Lah, wa ashhadu anna Muhammadu Rasool-Allah: "I bear witness that there is no deity except God, and I bear witness that Muhammad is the Messenger of God," the Declaration of Faith or *Shahadah*.

Ayah (plural, *ayat*): a verse of the Qur'an; also, a sign (of God).

Bismillahi-r-Rahmani-r-Raheem: in the name of God, the Most Merciful, the Most Compassionate.

Dajjal: literally, "deceiver"; the Anti-Christ, a satanic imposter who will appear in the End Time to lead people to a false religion, and who will be killed by Jesus (࿈) at his second coming

Dhikr (or *dhikr-Allah*): the remembrance of God, generally through repetition of phrases of glorification, certain of His holy Names, or verses of the Qur'an.

Dhul-Hijjah: the twelfth month of the Islamic calendar, the month of the pilgrimage (*hajj*).

Dua: literally, "calling" (upon God); personal, private prayer or supplication.

Eid: festival.

Eid al-Adha: the Festival of Sacrifice, which falls during the time of the pilgrimage (*hajj*).

Eid al-Fitr: the Festival of Fast-Breaking following Ramadan.

Futoor (*iftar*): breaking the fast at sunset at the end of a day of fasting.

Gabriel (Arabic, *Jibreel*): the archangel who brought God's revelations to the prophets.

Ghusl: literally, "washing"; the major ablution or shower which becomes obligatory when one is in a state of major pollution.

Habeeb: beloved.

Hadith: reports of the Prophet's words and deeds.

Hajj: the prescribed pilgrimage to Mecca.

Halal: permissible, allowed, lawful according to Islamic law.

Haram: prohibited, forbidden, unlawful according to Islamic law.

Hijab: veil, cover, screen; in common usage, the covering of the Muslim woman.

Hijrah: migration, specifically the emigration of Prophet Muhammad (ﷺ) from Mecca to Medina in the year 622 CE; the anniversary of this migration on the first of the month of Muharram marks the Islamic New Year.

Iftar: see *Futoor*.

Ihsan: that which is more admirable, splendid and excellent.

Imam: leader; specifically, the leader of the prayer (*salat*), who also delivers the sermon during the Friday prayer and the prayers of the two festivals (*Eid*s).

Iman: faith, belief.

Islam: literally, "peace, submission, surrender" to God; in this text, "*islam*" denotes the original religion revealed by God through all the prophets, while "Islam" denotes the final, universal faith revealed through the prophet Muhammad (ﷺ).

Jinn: an ordinarily invisible order of beings created of fire; Satan is the chief of the evil *jinn*.

Jumah: Friday.

Kabah: literally, "cube"; the sacred House of God in Mecca, built by the prophets Abraham and Ishmael (ﷺ), which Muslims face during their prayers and to which they go on pilgrimage.

La ilaha illa-Llah: there is no deity except God.

Lailat al-Qadr: the Night of Power.

Mahdi: the divinely-appointed Guide whose coming in the latter days of this world to defeat the powers of evil and bring about the reign of righteousness was foretold by Prophet Muhammad (ﷺ).

Mahr: the dower or marriage gift given by a man to his bride.

Masjid: mosque, the Muslim place of worship.

Muhammadu Rasool-Allah: Muhammad is the Messenger of God.

Muharram: the first month of the Islamic lunar calendar; see *Hijrah*.

Muslim: in this text, "*muslim*" denotes people of pre-Islamic times who were in a state of *islam* or surrender to God, while "*Muslim*" denotes a follower of the faith of Islam revealed through Prophet Muhammad (ﷺ). The root letters *s-l-m* connect the meaning of this word with the meaning of the word "*islam*".

Muta: temporary, conditional marriage, prohibited in Islam.

Nabi: literally, "one who brings news" (from God); a prophet, one who is specially appointed and trained by God to convey His revelations and guidance.

Nafs: self or soul; the lower self or ego (*nafsa la-ammara bis-sou*), that part of the self which commands evil, is also commonly referred to as the *nafs*.

Rabiul-Awwal: the third month of the Islamic calendar; the Prophet's birthday is on the twelfth of this month.

Rakat: a cycle or unit of prayer (*salat*); each prayer is made up of a fixed number of *rakats*.

Ramadan: the ninth month of the Islamic lunar calendar, the month of fasting.

Rasool: a messenger—that is, a prophet who was given a divinely-revealed scripture by God.

Salat (*salah* or *namaz*): the prescribed prayer.

Sawm (*siyam*): fasting.

Sehri: see *Suhoor*.

Shahadah: literally, "witnessing"; the Islamic Declaration of Faith.

Shariah (or *Shariat*): the sacred Law of Islam, derived primarily from the Holy Qur'an and the Prophet's *sunnah*, and secondarily from the consensus of early Islamic scholars and analogy.

Shawwal: the tenth month of Islamic calendar, which immediately follows Ramadan.

Suhoor: the pre-dawn meal on a day of fasting.

Sunnah: the practice or traditions of the Prophet (ﷺ).

Surah: a chapter of the Qur'an.

Taher: pure, clean.

Taqwa: consciousness or mindfulness of God.

Taraweeh: the special *salat* observed nightly during Ramadan.

Ummah: community or nation.

Wudu: the minor ablution which precedes *salat*.

Zakat (*zakah*): the obligatory poor-due.

GOOD READING ON ISLAM

THE HOLY QUR'AN

READINGS IN THE QUR'AN
  translation by Kenneth Cragg, Bell and Bain, U.K.—*selections from the Qur'an in modern English, arranged by topic.*

THE ESSENTIAL KORAN: THE HEART OF ISLAM
  by Thomas Cleary, Harper Collins Publishers, NY—*selections from the Holy Book in modern English.*

THE MEANING OF THE GLORIOUS KORAN
  translation by M. M. Pickthall—*one of the two most widely-read renditions into English.*

THE HOLY QUR'AN, TRANSLATION AND
COMMENTARY
  by A. Yusuf Ali—*one of the two most widely-read renditions into English.*

THE MESSAGE OF THE QUR'AN
  translations and commentary, by Muhammad Asad, Dar al-Andalus, Gibraltar—*an expanded rendition into English by a convert from Judaism, with an extensive, scholarly commentary.*

THE QUR'AN
  translation and commentary, by T. B. Irving, Amana Books, Brattleboro, VT—*a rendition into modern English by an American Muslim scholar.*

PROPHET MUHAMMAD

MUHAMMAD—HIS LIFE FROM THE EARLIEST
SOURCES
  by Martin Lings, Inner Traditions International, Rochester, VT—*a detailed account of the Prophet's life, written in a reverent, moving style.*

SUBMISSION—THE SAYINGS OF THE PROPHET
MUHAMMAD
  by Shems Friedlander, Harper Collins, San Francisco—*a book of selected hadiths of the Prophet (ﷺ).*

THE SAYINGS OF MUHAMMAD
  by A. A. Suhrawardy, Carol Publishing Group, Secaucus, NJ—*a selection of hadiths, arranged by topic.*

GENERAL INTEREST

ADHAN OVER ANATOLIA
by Marian Kazi, American Trust Publications, Plainfield, IN—
*the moving diary of an American Muslim living in Turkey during
the troubled '70s, with reflections on Iran and Pakistan.*

COVERING ISLAM
by Edward W. Said, Pantheon Books—*an important work for those
interested in understanding how the media transforms our thought.*

ISLAM AND THE DESTINY OF MAN
by Charles Le Gai Eaton, State University of New York Press,
Albany—*an in-depth discussion of Islam's universality and relevance to the contemporary world.*

ISLAM BETWEEN EAST AND WEST
by 'Alija 'Ali Izetbegovic, American Trust Publications,
Plainfield, IN—*written several years ago by the current president
of Bosnia-Herzegovina.*

ISLAM IN FOCUS
by Hammudah Abdalati, American Trust Publications,
Plainfield, IN—*a basic, well-written book on Islam.*

ISLAM, THE STRAIGHT PATH
by John Esposito, Oxford University Press, NY—*a balanced
analysis of Islamic thought, with emphasis on the historical and
political aspects of Muslim life.*

ISLAMIC THREAT—MYTH OR REALITY?
by John Esposito, Oxford University Press, NY—*a discussion of
current issues involving Muslim peoples.*

JESUS, A PROPHET OF ISLAM
by Muhammad 'Ata ur-Rahim, MWH London Publishers,
London, U.K.—*explores the life and teachings of the prophet
Jesus (*ﷺ*).*

THE AUTOBIOGRAPHY OF MALCOLM X
as told to Alex Haley, Grove Press, NY—*the famous book upon
which Spike Lee's film was based.*

THE BIBLE, THE QUR'AN, AND SCIENCE
by Maurice Bucaille, Seghers, Paris—*an intriguing comparison
of the findings of modern science with passages from the Bible
and the Qur'an.*

THE CHILDREN'S BOOK OF SALAH
by Ghulam Sarwar, The Muslim Educational Trust, London—

one of the easiest and most complete books for learning the prayer, suitable for either children or adults.

THE CONCISE ENCYCLOPEDIA OF ISLAM

by Cyril Glasse, Harper and Row Publishers, San Francisco—*a comprehensive and extremely useful reference work covering a multitude of topics.*

THE DEAD SEA SCROLLS, THE GOSPEL OF BARNABAS, AND THE NEW TESTAMENT

by M. A. Yusseff, American Trust Publications, Plainfield, IN—*an insightful account of the origins of Pauline Christianity, contrasted with the Dead Sea Scrolls and the lost gospel of the apostle Barnabas.*

THE HADJ—AN AMERICAN'S PILGRIMAGE TO MECCA

by Michael Wolfe, Atlantic Monthly Press, NY—*a well-written account of an American Muslim's hajj.*

THE VISION OF ISLAM

by Sachiko Murata and William Chittick, Paragon House, NY— two eminent scholars explore practice, faith, spirituality and the Islamic view of history.

UNVEILING ISLAM

by Roger du Pasquier, Islamic Texts Society, Cambridge, UK—a sympathetic exposition of Islamic beliefs and practices from a Westerner's point of view view.

These books and many others, as well as a selection of Islamic videos, are available from the sources listed below (catalogs available on request):

KAZI Publications, Inc., 3023 W. Belmont Ave., Chicago, IL 60618. Tel. 312-267-7001, FAX 312-267-7002.

Islamic Books Service, 2622 E. Main St., Plainfield, IN 46168. Tel. 317-839-8150, FAX 317-839-2511.

IBTS, P. O. Box 5154, New York, NY 11105. Tel. 718-721-4246, FAX 718-728-6108.

Soundvision, 843 W. Van Buren, Suite 411, Chicago, IL 60607. Tel. 312-226-0205, FAX 312-226-7537.

GENERAL INDEX

A
Aaron, 33, 35
abortion, 107
Abraham, 7, 26, 31, 33-34, 37, 40, 70, 81, 85, 137, 140
accountability, 4, 10, 18, 32, 42, 88, 113, 117-118
acts of worship, 24, 30, 69-82, 105, 128
Adam, 7, 10, 32-33, 35, 37, 39, 92, 132, 135-140, 143
adultery, 98, 112
Ahmad, 37, 138
Aisha, 46, 142
alcohol, 23, 66, 100-101, 141
Allah, 136
angel(s), 20-21, 24-27, 41-42, 45-46, 51-52, 56, 70, 78, 86, 95, 127, 136-137, 143
Angel of Revelation, 25, 27, 41, 78, 86
anger, 53, 57, 59, 64, 91, 119, 128, 132, 138
animal(s), 19, 21, 29, 34, 85, 103, 121
Anti-Christ, 38
Arabic, 19, 25, 28, 30-31, 70, 75, 83-84, 128, 135-139
Arafat, Plain of, 85
Armageddon, 2
Article(s) of Faith, 15, 24, 31, 48, 58
astrology, 100

B
attributes, God's, 15, 18, 28, 39, 60, 90, 129

backbiting, 80, 100
bad deeds, 52, 55, 77
behavior, 1-2, 79, 87, 91, 95-103, 115, 121, 124
belief, 5-7, 12, 15, 24-26, 31, 34, 38, 47-48, 56, 65-66, 70, 72, 126-127, 132, 134
beliefs, 6, 13, 15-69, 87, 95, 125, 131
believer(s), 34, 45, 48, 58, 87, 113, 125, 139, 142
Bible, 26-27
birthday, Prophet's, 86
bleeding, 75, 80, 106-107
blood, 43, 106, 109-110, 122
body, 17, 19-20, 45, 50, 52, 73, 78, 89, 105-106, 110, 113-114, 121-122, 133, 139
Books, revealed, 26-31, 141
breast-feeding, 80, 115, 119
bribery, 43, 98, 100
brotherliness, 93

C
calamity(ies), 58-62, 64, 66, 129, 139
calendar, Islamic, 78, 81, 84, 86
call to prayer, 71
certainty, 1, 4-5, 28, 42, 47-48, 52, 63, 74, 76, 89, 126-127

Friday prayer, 83, 140

G

Gabriel, Angel, 25, 27-28, 41,
    45, 70, 78, 86, 127, 137
ghusl, 83, 106-107
generosity, 91, 123
glorification of God, 69, 71,
    73, 83, 141
God, 5-10, 12-13, 15-51, 53-
    67, 69-74, 76-84, 86-93, 95-
    100, 102, 105, 109-114, 116-
    120, 123, 125-127, 129-143
god(s) 22-23, 40, 70, 136-137
good, 1, 18, 23, 26, 52-55, 57-
    59, 64-65, 67, 72, 74, 76,
    90, 93, 96-97, 101-102, 119,
    123, 126, 128-129, 132-133,
    142
good deeds, 52-56, 80
goodness, 38, 52-53, 56, 59,
    61, 119-120, 128-129, 134
good news, 32, 37, 46, 66
grace, God's, 39-40, 58
guardian, 111
guidance, 6-7, 9, 12-13, 22,
    26, 28, 31-34, 43, 46, 55-56,
    71-72, 78-79, 87, 123, 132,
    134, 136
Guided One, 38

H

hadith(s), 25, 30, 38, 46-47,
    56, 91, 100-102, 126-127,
    134, 138-142

hajj, 69-70, 81-82, 85
halal, 97, 100, 110
haram, 4, 97, 100, 110
harm, 4, 55, 92, 100, 107,
    132
harmful, 4-5, 22, 97, 103,
    128-129, 132, 141
health, 62-63, 81, 88, 133
heart(s),2-3, 5-6, 17, 19, 28,
    32, 42, 52, 54, 56-57, 59,
    63, 72, 89-92, 102, 111, 125-
    126, 128, 130, 133
Heaven, 47-58, 140
Hell, 25, 47-58, 133
help, God's, 6, 45, 60, 65-66,
    74, 83, 88, 129-130
helpfulness, 90, 92, 114, 120
Hereafter, 10-11, 22, 28, 42,
    47-58, 61, 65, 72, 96, 110
hijab, 121-122
hijrah, 44, 86
Hira Cave, 41, 78, 86
Holy Spirit, 28, 36, 137
home, 44, 50, 63, 71, 75, 79,
    88, 106, 115-117, 122-123
homosexuality, 98
honesty, 41, 99
honor, 6, 24, 35, 89-92, 98,
    111, 121, 130, 132, 134, 141
hope, 8, 46
hospitality, 91
House of God, 40, 82, 140
housework, 116, 142
human nature, 3, 18-21, 49,
    54, 96